MW01172584

Thou Shall Not Be Emotionally Wounded

_____

_____

_____

_____

_____

_____

_____

_____

_____

_____

_____

_____

_____

_____

_____

_____

_____

Prison is full of people with active pain-bodies seeking to be fed.

A volunteer with an active pain-body runs the dangerous risk of what I call "emotional cannibalism." Your wounds feed the prisoner, and the prisoner's wounds feed you... and holy hell breaks loose.

Thus, the fourth commandment of prison ministry is *Thou Shall Not Be Emotionally Wounded.* Now you see why.

This leads us to the fifth commandment: *Thou Shall Not Seek Approval.*

The Risk That it Took to Blossom: Deep Dive Devotionals on Growing Through Grief
By Nicole Luciana Cagna

Dedication: I would first like to dedicate this book to Father God, Jesus Christ, and Holy Spirit. Without Your Love and Guidance, these words might have been locked forever inside my heart, searching desperately for a page to land on.

I would also like to thank my amazing husband, Chris, who has been and continues to be the Love of my Life, and everything I asked the Lord for in a husband plus some! You are my best friend and I can't imagine one single day without you.

Lastly, I would like to thank my son, Christian. You have been my sunshine on the darkest of days. You are a special vessel. God gave us you and for that I am so incredibly grateful.

To the One Who is Grieving,

I will never forget the days after my daughter Eve passed away. I remember feeling numb as I was wheeled from the Hospital to the car, a balloon my parting gift. I should have gone home with one pink balloon and one blue balloon, but instead, there was only blue that day. One blue balloon. I limped through the door with pain due to an emergency C-section and a blood transfusion. The house was a disaster as my husband was at Westchester Medical monitoring, Eve. Grief. I walked through the door in a haze with one baby, when my body yelled at me that I had two. Grief. I could not bring myself to take any phone calls or hear congratulations in the same breath as apologies for my loss. I could not care that they were offended by my lack of communication.

As I struggled through the memorial service for my daughter and taking care of my son, I found grief to be elusive. After the numb stage, I just became angry. I was angry at a God of miracles who felt that Eve would be better off in Heaven. I was angry that my first pregnancy went this way. I was angry that this happened to our family after we had already been through so much. Mostly, I was angry that the world went on spinning when my life was falling apart. This did not feel like the victorious Christian life I was meant to lead.

The Lord inspired me to channel my grief into writing what I experienced and learned through this trying journey. There are so many layers of healing in this devotional book. I pray the healing Balm of Gilead over your heart as you read it. Grief is raw and real and we don't have to package it with a pretty bow to make others feel better about our pain. Know that this devotional is a safe place for your heart wherever you are on this journey.

In Compassion,
Your companion, Nicole L. Cagna

Table of Contents

Sections

"Still"

Just be still
Sit at my feet
It's not over
It's not defeat

This is deeper
This is filling
Just be present
Just be willing

Feel the dry bones
Watch them grow
Feel the deep groans
Let tears flow

There is healing
In deeper places
There is feeling
Within numb spaces

An army grown
From bones in earth
An army sown
And given birth

By my Spirit
You will be whole
You need not fear it
I'm in control

For now just rest
In my embrace
I know what's best
Just seek my face

You're meant to fly
I'll fix your wing
You're meant to roar
I'll teach you to sing

Be the flower
Embrace the thorn
Receive my power
Release the scorn

I prepared this season
For you to learn
It's for this reason

It's now your turn

To walk into your destiny
Travel land that may seem bare
In order to set the captives free
You must first journey there

The promised land is flowing
The milk and honey sweet
I'll train you to slay giants
You will not know defeat

So rest my weary soldier
Let me fill you overflowing
Just be held and trust me
I know where you're going

Written by Nicole Luciana Cagna

The Triumph of Tears

"When they walk through the Valley of Weeping, it will become a place of refreshing springs. The autumn rains will clothe it with blessings." Psalm 84:6

"What do YOU want"? The Lord asked me as I cried out to Him in the midnight hour. I told Him what I had told Him for the last seven years, "I want YOUR will for my life, Lord." There was silence for a moment and then, "No, what do YOU want"? He asked again. I became frustrated, and my response was the same. The third time He said again, "Nicole, what do YOU want?". Something broke inside of me and tears began to flood my eyes. Everything was blurry, and I felt undone by the simplest question. I said hoarsely through the frog in my throat, "I want another baby, a girl. Okay??? Are you happy now?" There was silence for another moment as the gravity of what just happened set in. He said, "Now, the healing can begin." The truth is my mind does not want another baby at all. I am weary, and when I pray, I ask for my physical healing so I can be free. I ask for my son to be healed from the autism diagnosis, this sneaky condition that can sometimes cause him to behave in ways that make him unrecognizable to me. The last thing my mind wants is another child. I look at the natural factors and facts that I am thirty-nine, and my body needs complete healing. I look at how difficult it is to raise a child on the spectrum. Naturally, I can't fathom doing this all over again. In fact, the odds are impossible in the natural realm. Here I was called out on a desire that my mind refused to let my heart have. God knew. My life is His, and I don't want to receive anything that He doesn't want for me. I know that what He has is infinitely better. But, I turned that into something it should never have been: avoidance. There is an epic battle between my mind and my heart. I am both left brained and right brained equally, and I am not one who relies on my feelings. I remember waking up one day and thinking, "Where are my dreams? What are my goals?" I wondered what happened to the young woman who thought about the future and was excited about what God was going to do. Sometimes we become so weary in our present circumstances that are living a life of mere existence. We are surviving not thriving. There is a numbness that becomes comfortable, and we use it to protect ourselves against the pain of God saying, "No".

The Lord was showing me through this verse in Psalms that even the earth weeps. I always thought it strange that after a brutal winter with snow, Spring was full of rain. Why the rain before the flowers? Wasn't the snow enough? The cold, bitter winds and temperatures that make us want to hibernate are gone, why celebrate with rain? The rain is the gap between the old season and the new. Between seasons the earth weeps and her tears birth flowers and beauty beyond belief. How much easier would it be if after the cold winter we could just experience Spring? How much easier if we could just shed this old season like snakeskin and move past the transition into our new season? The reality is that we can't. The old season of winter and it's melting snow could never sustain the flowers for the spring season. No, there must be fresh water, fresh tears to cultivate the land for what is about to happen, to sustain the new season.

The Holy Spirit then led me to this verse. The Valley of Baca was a dry and parched land. Translations have been argued, but the root word means weeping. The Valley of Baca was known as a land of lamentation and also means to "properly weep." It was a place that had to be passed through to head to Zion. It could not be avoided. In this valley, passengers would dig holes in the ground and make wells to catch the rain that would fall. Because it was such a dry place it did not rain. So, the rain the Psalmist used was a metaphor for God's provision during the journey through the valley. We need reminders as we travel the valley looking for relief that God's blessings and promises will be our comfort. We don't realize how our tears in the natural can create an oasis for the next weary passenger to drink from. In the dark night of the soul, we feel God is hiding from us, and we are facing attacks from the Enemy, as well as other afflictions. It's easy to feel isolated and ashamed of our struggles as if we are "too mature" to have such feelings and afflictions. When we allow that mindset to enter into our spirits, we are just building a wall of protection, so we aren't hurt. Instead of digging INTO the ground we build OFF OF the ground. Instead of digging into the deeper healing God wants to do we attempt to protect ourselves from it because it hurts. It's hard to embrace this time in our lives, but we must "properly weep" to make room for more of Him. This is the gap between the old and the new, the space between the valley and the mountain top. We must be willing to endure the valley because that is where we learn perseverance. It is where we are malleable enough to receive the presence and power of God. It is where His anointing for our destiny is imparted.

That night, God called me out. Having desires and dreams for your life is not a bad thing. We are not robots. To protect myself from disappointment, I was simply avoiding acknowledging that I had any desires or dreams other than to be healed. It came from a place of loss. I desired and believed Eve would receive a miracle on earth, but He chose Heaven. I desired my full healing, but seven years later I am still waiting. I desired a son who was healthy in every way but received an autism diagnosis instead. I desired more children through IVF, but instead had to donate my embryos because of Addison's Disease. Over the years my desires and dreams have been crushed at every turn. It became easier to use the pat answer, "Thy Will be Done," and while I mean that when I say it, deep down I figured it was better to live that way so it wouldn't hurt so badly. So,He dug into the recesses of my heart and found a desire there, one I wish I didn't have. He is asking me to deal with the grief of the loss of my desires in this season. It's not enough that I just grieve Eve, but that I grieve the loss of a very personal and intimate dream. A dream that doesn't make sense. A desire that I can't control. It's okay to grieve the losses of what we hoped for. It doesn't mean we lack faith or trust in God. It means we are human. As long as we are willing to place aside what we want for what He wants, then we are honoring Him with our lives. As long as our dreams and desires don't become an idol that takes the place of God, we remain steadfast. Still, despite the pain of this season, it's important to remember the miracles in the middle of it all. God delivered me from death's door three times. He miraculously saved my life and the life of my son when science said we shouldn't be alive. I must choose to tell my soul to bless the Lord in this valley because it's a lonely place where it's easy to forget His goodness. I must allow myself to feel and avoid the desire to stay busy because there is a purpose for this pain, and am willing to find out what it is.

What are the lost dreams and desires that you have buried in the recesses of your heart? Ask the Holy Spirit to reveal them to you today, and begin to pray for them. Ask God to heal the broken pieces and restore what the locusts have eaten. Bring to light what it is you desire and ask your Father in Heaven for those things. Don't prepare yourself for disappointment, just trust that whatever the answer may be, it is for your benefit. Lastly, share your tale of tears, and don't let shame shut down a testimony that others can drink from. Let's get ready to dig.

Prayer Starter: Lord, I don't like this. I don't like this valley of weeping I am experiencing. I don't like the surgery being done on my heart, but I know it's for my benefit. Take these tears Lord and use them for Your benefit and my good. Let them be sown now into the new season so it can be sustained and strong. Show me the holes to dig so I can go and grow even deeper in You. I thank You that You are with me whether in the Valley or on the Mountain. Though my tears may flow, and my feelings fluctuate, You are the unchanging God! In Jesus' name, I pray, Amen.

Cradling the Cup

"Then Jesus went with them to the olive grove called Gethsemane, and he said, "Sit here while I go over there to pray." He took Peter and Zebedee's two sons, James and John, and he became anguished and distressed. He told them, "My soul is crushed with grief to the point of death. Stay here and keep watch with me."He went on a little farther and bowed with his face to the ground, praying, "My Father! If it is possible, let this cup of suffering be taken away from me. Yet I want your will to be done, not mine."Then he returned to the disciples and found them asleep. He said to Peter, "Couldn't you watch with me even one hour? Keep watch and pray, so that you will not give in to temptation. For the spirit is willing, but the body is weak!"Then Jesus left them a second time and prayed, "My Father! If this cup cannot be taken away unless I drink it, your will be done." When he returned to them again, he found them sleeping, for they couldn't keep their eyes open.So he went to pray a third time, saying the same things again. Then he came to the disciples and said, "Go ahead and sleep. Have your rest. But look—the time has come. The Son of Man is betrayed into the hands of sinners. Up, let's be going. Look, my betrayer is here!" Matthew 26:36-44

Our little family was out for dinner at our favorite burger place a few nights back. On the drive home I was telling my husband about this video I saw about a pregnant couple who just gave birth to a newborn little girl. Everything was going well the first few hours until her heart started failing and a multitude of other problems began to arise. This couple of Faith believed in God's healing and proclaimed the miracle that God would heal their little girl. The doula even received a vision from God of Jesus showing up and laying His hand on the newborn's heart. Immediately her heart started pumping again, and her lungs which had collapsed righted themselves. Doctors could not believe the X-Rays and many staff became saved from this testimony. My eyes began to tear up, and I said to my husband, Chris, "Must have been nice." He knew what I meant. In no way were we minimizing the family's trying event. We were speaking of how nice it would have been for Eve to be healed on earth as well. The similarity of our stories was uncanny but the endings so much different. With tears in my eyes, I began to share how I felt. My five-year-old son who was quiet and must have been listening said, "He collects every tear, Mommy." Of course, this led to more tears flowing down my face, but it also allowed me to meditate on the common denominator of both encounters. Jesus showed up. So many times we base our Faith on the outcome of the tragedy, but is that really Faith?

When we pray in the midst of tragedy and say "Thy will be done" do we mean it? Because if we did, then wouldn't we be able to accept His answer no matter what it was? What if our Faith was based not on the outcome of what we expect but that Jesus shows up at all? When we pray, we have an expectation, but often we place significance in the outcome of what we ask. If the outcome differs at all from what we want, then our faith is shaken like a tree without roots. What if our Faith was based on the expectation that when tragedy strikes Jesus will show up, period? Our assurance is that we serve a God who carries us, loves us, and strengthens us. This is what our Faith should be based on, but I propose we have a problem in our walks and it's called conditional faith. When our faith is conditional, it affects the way we see God, Jesus, and the Holy Spirit. We perceive prayers answered in the way we want indicates that God is for us and we walk more confidently in our faith. When God allows us to struggle through the storms of life, we can easily perceive Him as punishing us, rejecting us, or simply ignoring us. This is the problem with conditional faith; it tells us that God's character changes and with an unstable perception of God our faith loses stability as well. I know what it feels like to completely surrender to His will and still walk through the pain of what that looks like. I think well-meaning Christian pollute this truth a bit when giving cavalier quotes intended to make us feel better about the cup of suffering. It's easy to be the cheerleader for the family who has their lips to that cup, but trying to swallow the contents of that cup is a different story entirely.

Jesus understood what the cup of suffering was. He knew the torture and agony before Him and asked not once or twice, but three times if the cup of suffering could be passed. He asked if there was any other way to accomplish the work of the cross other than enduring it. There wasn't, and worse was that His friends who were supposed to intercede for Him while He spoke to His Father fell asleep. Jesus felt completely alone, but in faith said: "Thy will be done". He didn't say it as a phrase to let God the Father know how religious He was or in false piety or some form of humility. No, Jesus meant that even if His own Father allowed Him to endure this suffering and the brief separation, He would do so. Now let's remember that Jesus at any time could have stopped what was happening. He had the power to stop His crucifixion. What kept Jesus on that cross was obedience. Jesus' obedience even unto death was based on intimacy with the Father. He knew that if Father God allowed Him to be sacrificed for us, then there was no other way. He trusted His Father, knew that He was still loved, even when He felt forsaken.

Matthew and Mark describe the last words of Jesus as "Eli, Eli, lama sabachthani?" meaning "Father, Father why have you forsaken me? The torture of being apart from His Father along with the physical and mental anguish of what He was feeling as the weight of the world's sins burdened His shoulders in those last breaths was overwhelming. If Jesus felt such anguish then how can we honestly expect not to? John describes the last words of Jesus as "It is finished." Some felt that this meant Jesus was saying his life was ending, but instead Jesus was referring to His mission. His mission was completed. He drank of the cup of suffering with all of its sour vinegar and finished what He set out to do in obedience. Luke describes the last words of Jesus as "Father into your hands I commit my spirit." Still, even after the road that Jesus chose to travel, He trusted His Father, committing His spirit into the hands of the one He loved and trusted. We have this expectation that a loving God would never ask us to endure the pain of losing a child, a spouse, a disease, a hard marriage, a beloved pet. Those are the very things that refine us and stretch us into our purpose and destiny. A little girl cannot fit into a woman's dress, just like our character at times cannot fit into the size of our call, so we must grow and stretch so that we can wear that call seamlessly.

At the end of the day, my desire will always be that I wish Eve was a healthy five-year-old girl giving her brother an attitude and some sass. Just like your desire will always be to have the one you loved and lost sitting next to you while you read this. These are not wrong things to desire. Jesus outright asked that the cup of suffering be passed from Him. The defining moment is that He accepted the cup anyway even though He had the power to change it. I know what I would do if I had the power to change it like Jesus. I would not have stayed on that cross. You wouldn't either. That's okay; we are not meant to be Jesus. There is only one Jesus! The truth is that I still trust God and love Him. I know that this cup of suffering my husband and I have had to drink from several times, doesn't mean that I am forgotten or forsaken and it doesn't mean you are either. It means that God gives us the grace to endure the sip, persevere in committing our lives into His hands, and when our life's mission is complete to say, "It is finished" knowing that it is just the beginning.

Prayer Starter: Father I want this cup to be passed from my lips, and I feel I just can't take another sip. Please cover me in your grace and strength to endure what you are allowing to refine me and mold me into the destiny You have for me. When I am weary, Lord let Your joy be my strength, when I feel I can't take another step, remind me that You are the one who orders those steps. When I am broken and weary let me hand You the pieces committing them into Your capable hands, Lord, Thank you, Lord, in Your Name, Amen.

Our Portion His Presence

When I was a little girl, my cousin and I were only a few years apart, so he was more like a little brother to me. I remember one day, a boy that we were friends with turned on him. I couldn't find him, and school had just let out. I was around seven years old, and he was five. I called his name and then heard whimpering in the alley of our school. There was my little cousin with his face in the dirt a tear streaked his face clearing the dirt away while his arm was bent back as this other boy sat on him. I don't remember much else after that except the fact that I marched over there with my uniform skirt on, lifted him with one hand and threw him off of my cousin and into a fence. Needless to say, the bully ran away as I helped my cousin up while wiping the dirt off of him. I was infuriated. I never realized I had this justice button until more situations came across my plate as I grew older and I began defending the helpless. The justice button seems altruistic. When we think about it, we can feel like the superhero coming to the rescue of the helpless, and in a movie that would be great. It's not a movie, and a hero already came to die on the cross and defeat Death. I'm not saying we should ignore those who are oppressed. We all are called to stand up for what is right when we see a wrong. We just have to be very careful about that justice button because when it gets out of balance, it comes back to bite you.

Fast forward decades later, and my husband and I were married only a few months. I didn't like the way he was being treated in a certain area of his life. It affected me so much that instead of praying for it, I began to think how to fix it for him. I spent hours thinking about it, and wasted energy angry about it. That anger turned into bitterness towards that area, and it was becoming harder to show grace. My husband said to me after dinner one night, "You know this is affecting you more than it is me." I thought about that and realized he was right. I couldn't get justice for my husband, and God wasn't doing it as fast as I wanted to, and so while waiting, I became bitter.

In our suffering series part one, we talked about the release of tears and its afflictions so that we may grow in Christ rather than protecting ourselves. We discussed the suppression of lost dreams and desires so we wouldn't hear God's answer if it was "No". In the second part of the series, "Cradling the Cup," we shared the importance of knowing the character of God when encountering tragedy, so that when we do say "Thy Will Be Done" we say it trusting that whatever the outcome our faith will remain unshaken. However, it's important to show also, the importance of HOW to wait because it is when we are hurting the most that we decide to take matters into our own hands and look around at who is living a better life.

I would struggle with this justice button for decades when I saw situations that were unjust in others' lives until, like Asaph, I had to walk through my own season of injustice with situations that kept hitting my husband and I like meteorites crashing into our lives creating large holes. In Psalm 73, Asaph goes through a crisis of Faith during a time of great suffering. We can learn a lot from Asaph in this Psalm.

This is Not Fair

Psalm 7: 1- 3 says,

**" Truly God is good to Israel,
to those whose hearts are pure.
But as for me, I almost lost my footing.
My feet were slipping, and I was almost gone.
For I envied the proud
when I saw them prosper despite their wickedness."**

When things happen in our lives that are unfair and tragic, it is easy to lose our faith. After receiving the phone call from the doctor in Westchester that Eve died while I was receiving a blood transfusion in Orange County, the phone rang again. It was our mortgage company telling us that they would not work with us on our mortgage. Chris tried to explain that our daughter just died and the lady on speaker said, "I'm sorry sir, but that is not our problem we need to talk about your mortgage." At that moment I felt like my foot was slipping too. I thought "This is what following the Lord looks like? All of these attacks?". I looked at the wicked around me prospering despite their actions. It didn't seem fair, and it made me wonder if I should give up. This is a natural part of suffering in a season. It doesn't make you a bad Christian; it makes you human. It does, however, teach us a valuable lesson on keeping our eyes on our own lane. Our measure is not another's life. Our measure is Jesus Christ. We get into trouble when we begin comparing our lives with the lives of others. It doesn't matter whether they are saved or unsaved, naughty or nice. Other people's lives are not and will never be the way we must measure His goodness. Our measure is Jesus, and our portion is dispensed by Him and Him alone. Asaph began slipping when he started looking at how the wicked were living rather than focusing on God.

They Have it So Much Better

In Psalm 73:4-14 Asaph goes on to keep looking at the wicked and their prosperity until verse 13.

"They seem to live such painless lives;
their bodies are so healthy and strong.
They don't have troubles like other people;
they're not plagued with problems like everyone else.
They wear pride like a jeweled necklace
and clothe themselves with cruelty.
 These fat cats have everything
their hearts could ever wish for!
 They scoff and speak only evil;
in their pride, they seek to crush others.
 They boast against the very heavens,
and their words strut throughout the earth.
 And so the people are dismayed and confused,
drinking in all their words.
 "What does God know?" they ask.
"Does the Most High even know what's happening?"
 Look at these wicked people—
enjoying a life of ease while their riches multiply.

Did I keep my heart pure for nothing?
Did I keep myself innocent for no reason?
 I get nothing but trouble all day long;
every morning brings me pain."

Verse thirteen is what happens when we focus on something other than God. Asaph begins to ask whether or not this Christian walk is worth it. He's saying, " Am I doing all this work to be pure for nothing? Where is the payoff?". This is the danger of comparing ourselves to others in a season of suffering. When we do so, everything looks better than where we are, and an entitled mindset begins to form. Do we keep our covenant of purity with God for a return? We start to use business terms in a relational setting. That never works. Keeping our heart pure, protecting our heart is a vital part to our survival, but the mindset of entitlement doesn't care about that. Its gains are measured in the prosperity of the flesh when a clean heart is the true priceless treasure.

Wrestling With Why

Asaph realizes in Psalm 73 verses 15-16 the importance of keeping these thoughts to himself to wrestle privately. This is not to say we shouldn't share our problems, but that when we wrestle with God in Spirit, we must be careful about sharing those questionable thoughts with the younger in Christ. It may distract them and mislead their train of thought,

 "If I had really spoken this way to others,
I would have been a traitor to your people.
 So I tried to understand why the wicked prosper.
But what a difficult task it is!"

Instead, Asaph then tried to figure out the answer that only God could know; WHY? This is the question we always ask when in a season of suffering. All this did was frustrate Asaph more. I remember asking the same question about Eve and other tragic circumstances in my life. I couldn't believe that my diligence and strength and Faith didn't buy me a get out of jail free card. I knew that I wouldn't be skating in life and I would be attacked, but this amount of tragedy in such a short time made me question a lot too. Here's the answer; only God knows the answer. That is the truth of it. Asaph saw the futility of the question as he wrestled with God on the matter and so should we. That question can never fill us with the peace we think it will, only the Holy Spirit can do that. The question of why can become a convenient distraction if we let it.

Part Four of Our Portion His Presence will continue with Asaph's journey with suffering.

In the meantime ask yourself:

What do I consider unfair about my life?
What is my justice button?
Who else am I comparing my circumstances to? Who do I feel has it much better?
What is my Why? Write out your why question to God. Is this "why question" becoming my idol? Has it taken over my life? Does it affect my mood and decisions? Does it distract me from my purpose?

Prayer Starter: Father heal my heart today and use circumstances to honor You. Forgive me for comparing my life to another's and for envying what others have. I have no right to judge their walk. Instead, I should focus on my own walk with You. Take my why and change it to how. How will You use this Lord? Get me excited about my future and keep me focused on Your Word. Show me what You want for my life, Lord. In Your Precious and Holy Healing Name I pray, Amen.

Our Portion His Presence

In Part three of our Suffering Series, we talked about Asaph's response to his suffering. We talked about the first steps when we experience suffering. First, we say it's not fair and grieve our circumstances. Second, we look at others we consider undeserving and think that they have it much better. Lastly, we ask God the famous question of Why? I remember feeling all of those things too. Looking back on my circumstances it seemed entirely unfair that God who encouraged me to pursue the painful process of In Vitro would then allow Eve to die and a nasty disease to take her place. I used to look at the news where little children and babies were abused and neglected by their parents and cry because I would do anything to hold and love that child. In my mind, those people had it better because they at least were able to have children. Now, I see how warped that viewpoint was, but when looking through grief's lenses, it made sense. Lastly, I asked Why? I spent hours crying out to God asking why, but why was not going to give me the relief I sought. The deception of why is that if it is answered, we will become whole. The truth is that all loss must be grieved and the "why" does not fill the void we think it will. These are the stages we endure when grieving and it is natural. We still must guard our hearts because as the tears blur our eyes in the natural, they also can blur our spiritual eyes as well. I have found that after asking those questions and grieving the loss, nothing felt better. Only when I went seeking God and His Holy Spirit did I receive what I needed. Nothing changed in my circumstances, but my heart began to heal one beat at a time.

Revelation Revealed in Psalm 73:17-20

**"Then I went into your sanctuary, O God,
and I finally understood the destiny of the wicked.
Truly, you put them on a slippery path
and send them sliding over the cliff to destruction.
In an instant they are destroyed,
completely swept away by terrors.
When you arise, O Lord,
you will laugh at their silly ideas
as a person laughs at dreams in the morning."**

After visiting God's sanctuary, he understood that justice belonged to God and God alone. Asaph began to see the end demise of the wicked. The prosperity and happiness that is evident for us to see are fleeting. The truth is that those who live wickedly often have a sudden collapse for they have built their kingdom and rule it with their own hand. However legacy is not created in this false kingdom for once the false king is taken off of his throne, the rest returns to rubble. Comparing Kingdoms is ridiculous, and Asaph realizes that he serves a greater God, a God of destiny, legacy, and eternity.

The Bitter Truth in Psalm 73:21-22

"Then I realized that my heart was bitter,
and I was all torn up inside.
I was so foolish and ignorant—
I must have seemed like a senseless animal to you."

Conviction sets in when Asaph realized who and what he was envying. Have you ever had a vent session with God? I have. Sure, we call it prayer, and maybe some of it is, but really it's airing grievances in many ways when we are in a place of hopelessness. When we are hurting and nursing the wounds from places that have yet to be healed, the grass always looks greener. We see those without a care in the world living for themselves while our armor scuffed from battle longs for a place to rest our weary head. Asaph was angry and bitter at what the wicked had rather than discerning what they needed: God. Oh, how the Enemy uses the things that we don't have to distract us from the everyday blessings around us. With a heart of bitterness and anger, we look at all that we lack, grumbling about our inferiority, our finances, our children, our marriage, and in doing so we create roots of bitterness with seeds of ungratefulness invading our soil. We bring our rotten attitude and sense of entitlement before God and dare to call Him out calling it prayer. I, like Asaph, am grateful for the realization that comes through conviction.

Identity Restored in Psalm 73:23-25

"Yet I still belong to you;
you hold my right hand.
You guide me with your counsel,

leading me to a glorious destiny.
Whom have I in heaven but you?
I desire you more than anything on earth."

Asaph understood the most important thing to remember when in the midst of suffering: his identity. When we are hurting it is so easy to believe what the Enemy says about us. The truth is that we belong to God, and have the privilege of His wise counsel, love, and destiny. When we keep God on the throne where He belongs we find freedom. It is when we make our own suffering an idol that we get in trouble. A self-pity is a form of a victimhood mentality that can enslave us, convincing us that we are persecuted more than anyone else. The victimhood mentality keeps us in bondage and isolation. We become so consumed by our problems that we begin to question the character of God. When we restore God to His rightful place in the center of our lives our perspective changes, and we begin to see how cherished we truly are.

Trust Restored in Psalm 73:26

" My health may fail, and my spirit may grow weak,
but God remains the strength of my heart;
he is mine forever."

This particular verse hits home for me. As someone who has diagnoses of illnesses that I do not claim my own, the side effects can leave me weary and heavily fatigued. It's hard in those times to trust the Word of Healing God has spoken over my life. I have learned the hard way that my health can't become the measure of my strength. My health should not determine my attitude, and my fatigue should not dictate how good God is. The truth is our destiny, and our lives lived for Him are not based upon our health or weakness, but His strength. I remember doing prophetic ministry when my body was exhausted. I wondered how I would get through, but Holy Spirit showed up and took over. I was energized and full of His Spirit! This is not to say we ignore our body's cry for rest, but it means when God calls us to do something, His strength will sustain us. Knowing that we are His and that He is ours is comforting. When we allow the circumstances of our lives define us we get into trouble. He is the author and finisher of our faith and also the strength of our heart.

Testimony in Psalm 73:27-28

**"Those who desert him will perish,
for you destroy those who abandon you.
But as for me, how good it is to be near God!
I have made the Sovereign LORD my shelter,
and I will tell everyone about the wonderful things you do."**

Before losing Eve and finding illness I never wanted a dramatic testimony. In fact, I liked my testimony as it was thank you very much. I feared the suffering I would endure to gain that powerful testimony and I wanted no part of it. Who does? But the blood of the Lamb and the words of our testimony is how we overcome. Asaph realized that those who are not grafted into the Master Vine would perish, but then focused on his grafting. Asaph decided to stop looking at the story of lives played out before him and realized that his suffering was his testimony. Our testimony is not a story of sorrow but a vessel of victory. Yes, it hurts, and it's not easy, but it is powerful to see someone who has suffered be a vessel for the King. The key to testimony is not just surviving the scars, but relaying the revelation that God has released during the suffering. I see now that God has used my testimony to reach others who have experienced the loss of a child or are struggling with chronic illness. I see that although I am not where I want to be, I am not where I was. Only God can make beauty from ashes. Our testimony is a beacon of light and proof that only God can take something so unbearingly painful and birth something beautiful. As we share our testimony, we must focus less on the loss and more on God's glory. Even testimonies can be idols if it becomes our identity.

Jesus hung on the cross while most of His disciples hid in fear or watched from a distance. Judas betrayed Jesus for silver, the price of a slave. Job's friends in the midst of burying his children and boils insinuated that Job sinned thus deserving his punishment. It's never easy to experience things that aren't fair or just or right. Suffering is the great equalizer, as it does not care who it strikes, rich or poor. Suffering has this way of sifting relationships and creating a desperation for God's healing and in some cases vengeance.When suffering our eyes can begin to look at others who seem to have so much more going for them. We want their portion, not ours. It's so important while we are in our season of suffering not to become bitter as we wait for breakthrough and to remember that our portion is His presence.

Prayer Starter: Father, I thank You for who You are and what You are doing in my life. Sometimes, Lord, I compare where I am to where I want to be rather than looking at where I came from. Forgive me for my impatience, Lord, while waiting for Your promises. Forgive me for looking around rather than focusing on You. Forgive me for pressing on my justice button when You are the Judge, not me. Open my eyes to see and my ears to hear Your voice during this time of suffering. Let me be renewed by You, and refreshed by Your presence.Let me receive Your presence as my portion forever. In Your Name, Amen.

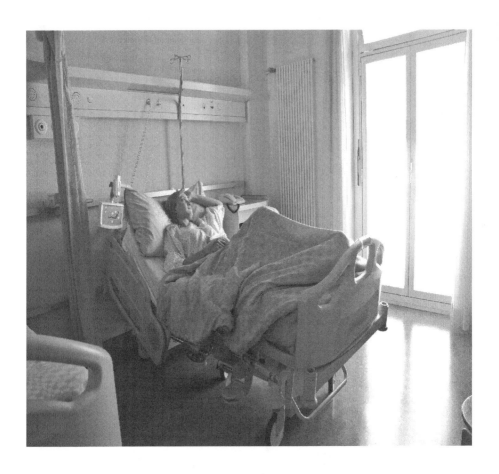

Remember the Restoration

"Remember Tobiah and Sanballat, my God, because of what they have done; remember also the prophet Noadiah and how she and the rest of the prophets have been trying to intimidate me. So the wall was completed on the twenty-fifth of Elul, in fifty-two days. When all our enemies heard about this, all the surrounding nations were afraid and lost their self-confidence, because they realized that this work had been done with the help of our God." Nehemiah 6:14-16

"Pulse dropping, heart rate 30. Blood pressure 30 over 40, run the IV QUICK". Slumped on a chair in my foyer, I could feel my body shutting down, my mind grasping to hold on to reality. The drops of blood on my tile floor were so red; I remember thinking. My husband kept Christian from looking as they loaded me onto the stretcher, "I love you" I croaked lamely. The ice pellets stung my skin as the paramedics made their way down our slippery driveway loading me into the ambulance. "I've never seen anything like that" the paramedic confided to me. "How are you conscious? That's not even possible. That's a miracle." he went on to confess. The ride to the ambulance was short, and I thought, "I remember...". The moment that I was fading, I knew that without my voice explaining to the Doctors about Addison's disease and what I needed, I would be left to die. I knew that because I often have to tell the doctors how to treat me. The medical bracelet would not speak loudly enough, and most likely they would not check. Chris had to stay back with Christian and drive him to my mother's house before meeting me at the Emergency Room. So, with all of this, while slumped over the chair, I whispered the most powerful name on the planet, "Lord." It was all the energy I had. Immediately, I saw the tops of trees and an open sky. There was a sun shining brightly. I saw His face come down from heaven out of that sun and rest his forehead on mine while He placed his hand on my head. At that moment I knew I would not pass out. I would not be left without a voice.

Once at the Emergency room, the doctor asked what happened, and I told him that I had a stomach bug that hit me suddenly and I went into adrenal crisis and then adrenal failure. They kept me for a few hours and then released me with extra steroids. My body was weak, and so I went home, and my husband took off of work to care for my little guy. I began to try and sort out my feelings of what occurred and what it meant. A stomach virus is not deadly for most people, yet the diagnosis of Addison's disease makes it so for me. I

31

began to remember how isolated and trapped I felt at that moment, and fear was born. I nearly died. Once that seedling sank in, I felt helpless and hopeless. Is this my life, Lord? Is this what it's going to be? How is this fulfilled? I began to forget about the moment He rested His forehead on mine, and the warm electric feeling of His powerful yet gentle hand on my head. I failed to remember the words of the paramedic. The word "miracle" was far from what I felt like. In fact, I felt betrayed. Betrayed by my body, betrayed by hope for a future without this disease. Suddenly, self-pity took over, and I felt victimized by a disease I could not control, a threat I could not see coming, and healing that was taking too long to arrive.

"Okay Lord" I grumbled, "Help me see You in this trial." I repented for my poor attitude and asked to see things through His lens, not my own. My lens was skewed, and because I felt like a victim, everything that happened made me look like one too. So, He began to remind me where He was in those moments and warned me about not connecting my past to my future. Battling with illness for the last seven years has been trying with hospital stays and emergency room trips, but even I could see how much healing has taken place in the last year despite the current circumstances. The Holy Spirit was reminding me to remember the restoration. I know it's so hard my sisters. Believe me, I know. Our fleshly nature speaks to us and says, "if the circumstances look the same they are the same." I assure you that is not the truth, and it is in fact deception. This deception is so dangerous because when you leave your starting point on this journey of growing in Him and becoming healed by Him, the Enemy wants you to believe you have been walking in place; that there has been no progress made. The circumstance looks the same; it feels the same, but it's NOT the same because you are NOT the same.

When Nehemiah rebuilt the wall, he received the same threats from day one of restoring the wall to day fifty-two of restoring the wall.

The threats were the same, the intimidation was the same, the Enemy was the same, but the wall was not the same, and Nehemiah was not the same. Nehemiah dealt with each threat, false prophecy, and more, yet still, restoration took place. I am sure that Nehemiah had to look at the progress of that wall, each new brick laid, each new level achieved, to be encouraged daily. We must do the same, reminding ourselves of the work His Spirit has done within our hearts, minds, spirits, and souls. God wants you and I to know that the circumstances do not dictate the restoration and growth in our lives, but rather how we persevere through those circumstances. We must protect the progressive work that God has done within us even when the outward circumstances say otherwise. We must also understand that many times these circumstances are actually a PART of our restorative process at a deeper level. So, here I am, resting in the knowledge that this moment will pass. I take a look at the tapestry of my life that He has so intricately woven together and I say, "Okay, Lord, I will remember the restoration and dive into the deeper level of healing" because this is how what is seemingly a burden becomes a blessing.

Prayer Starter: Lord, I thank you for my trials today because I know that it only means You are taking me deeper, deeper into Your Word, Your plan, and Your restoration. I know Lord that this season does not eradicate all the work You have done and all the progress that's been made, in fact, it will serve to move me forward Lord, into the destiny You have for me. I pray in this season as I sit at Your feet, you show me Your face and Your glory. Teach me Your ways, Oh Lord so that I may be filled. In Your Name, Amen.

The Risk of Restoration

"Then the family heads of Judah and Benjamin, and the priests and Levites—everyone whose heart God had moved—prepared to go up and build the house of the LORD in Jerusalem. All their neighbors assisted them with articles of silver and gold, with goods and livestock, and with valuable gifts, in addition to all the freewill offerings. Moreover, King Cyrus brought out the articles belonging to the temple of the LORD, which Nebuchadnezzar had carried away from Jerusalem and had placed in the temple of his god. Cyrus king of Persia had them brought by Mithredath the treasurer, who counted them out to Sheshbazzar the prince of Judah.This was the inventory: 10 gold bowls, 30 matching silver bowls, 410 other articles, 1,000. In all, there were 5,400 articles of gold and of silver. Sheshbazzar brought all these along with the exiles when they came up from Babylon to Jerusalem." Ezra 1: 5-11

I shared in one of my recent devotionals that I went into adrenal failure right before Christmas nearly dying. I didn't really understand the significance of the event until after it was revealed that I had to step back from my business, ministry, and more to take the time to recover. I put out notices letting the world know that my local and online skincare products would be on hold for a period of time. I let my Pastor know that I would be stepping back from ministry. Stepping back. Ugh. That word gets me. Stepping back just seemed like a nice way of saying "quit" in my eyes, yet I know that's not the truth, but it sure was how I felt. I still struggle seeing this season through God's eyes, but I am on this journey and I know that obedience is the first step. For so long I prayed for restoration of my health, our daughter we lost, everything that was stolen from us, so when this last bout of illness rolled over me, taking a step back seemed like a response to the illness rather than God's direction. How far from the truth that is. Is it possible that this sabbatical that God has given me is part of the path to receiving a deeper form of restoration?

In the book of Ezra, the Jewish captives knew all too well what it felt like to be removed from security and sent away in exile. They were a people without a home. King Cyrus was moved in his heart by God's Spirit to restore the Jewish people to their homes. He instructed neighbors to give offerings, silver, gold and more for this long and treacherous journey home. Furthermore, the Temple of God that was once destroyed was going to be rebuilt. King Cyrus took all the treasures that King Nebuchadnezzar stole out of the Temple and returned them to the Temple. This is the epitome of restoration. All that was lost and stolen was now going to be replaced. Yet Persian records show that though all the provision for the tumultuous journey home had been provided, many Jews stayed where they were. They had accumulated a lot of wealth in the area and moving would be too expensive, too dangerous, and too risky. Though they were still captives, the Persians had a relaxed policy towards the Jewish people. They were allowed to accumulate wealth, hold jobs, property and more. There was no pressing need to leave captivity and go home. In fact, going home was more work than ever. The Temple still needed to be rebuilt, and the Jewish people would have to start all over again. Restoration didn't look too good at that moment, so some chose to stay back and live in wealth and security rather than the required sacrifice necessary to complete their restoration.

I'm afraid to admit that I have done the same. While praying for restoration of the areas in my life where things were stolen from me, I developed quite the routine. I had a schedule, and things that I was doing in obedience to God, but then God flipped the script. Now, comes the work, the activity to help my limbs and joints heal physically, learning to deal with the feelings that come from tragic loss, learning to be still in His presence. This is work, this is the risk of restoration. I somehow believed that I would just wake up and restoration would smile and wave at me. I would be healed miraculously and whole in every area. So, while I have been on this long journey back to my Jerusalem, God has provided this time so that I may be whole. I can decide to be disobedient, and stay in my comfort zone, in my routine, but in doing so I would not really be free. I would still be a captive in a velvet prison. The truth is restoration never comes in the tidy package we'd like it to, and that's okay. It's the refinement of restoration that holds the most value.

What is your velvet prison? Are you choosing to stay in the comfort of captivity because it's the life you know? If so, I encourage you to leave all that you've built while in captivity and trade it in for the true refinement of restoration. He will meet you on that journey, and it will be worth it.

Prayer Starter: Father, I come before you today to say thank you for this refiner's fire. Thank you for this journey towards restoration. It may not look like I wanted it to, but I know that Your plans are infinitely better than mine. I know that my destiny awaits me in this journey. Reveal to me the places in my life where I am held captive, reveal the deception that has caused this bondage. I trade my captivity for freedom in all areas of my life, Lord. In Jesus' name, Amen.

The Return to Restoration

"With praise and thanksgiving they sang to the LORD: "He is good; his love toward Israel endures forever." And all the people gave a great shout of praise to the LORD, because the foundation of the house of the LORD was laid. But many of the older priests and Levites and family heads, who had seen the former temple, wept aloud when they saw the foundation of this temple being laid, while many others shouted for joy. No one could distinguish the sound of the shouts of joy from the sound of weeping, because the people made so much noise. And the sound was heard far away." Ezra 3:11-13

We pick up our story of Ezra in chapter three verses 11-13. In the last devotional you may have remembered that the Lord stirred King Cyrus' heart to allow the Jewish people to return home to Jerusalem. They were exiled in Persia at the time and had settled there accumulating wealth and positions. King Cyrus instructed neighbors to give freely money, food, wine, and other provisions for the treacherous four month journey. Many stayed back preferring the comfort of their captivity to the risk of restoration. Chapter three in Ezra picks up when the exiles that chose to return home begin the process of rebuilding the Temple. It took months upon months just to plan such a task and finally when the foundation of the Temple was laid there were mixed emotions. While the scripture states that ALL the people praised and worshiped the Lord, it was what happened after that which was defining. The older priests who had seen the former temple wept aloud. Why was that? The former Temple was that of Solomon which was far more ornate, surrounded by a thriving city and culture in a huge courtyard. Solomon's Temple had vast amounts of gold and precious stones. While close to the same size, the differences were obvious. This Temple was built amongst ruins. I would imagine that those who knew what it was like to have a Temple that looked like Solomon's were mourning that their disobedience took it away, while those who didn't know what it was like to have a Temple were thrilled. Perspectives regarding restoration vary.

I remember when I was in my early to mid twenties. I was healthy and in excellent shape, teaching High School English and working towards my Master's Degree. Looking at pictures of myself before illness, before the twins would cause me to tear up. I looked at that young woman in the picture and remembered her, but I also mourn her because I am not that woman anymore. In many ways it's a good thing. I am softer (both physically and emotionally) and more accessible. I love more, and have matured in ways that can only come from the Holy Spirit's ability to make beauty from ashes. I have another version of myself to compare myself to, and so when I am feeling badly because I can no longer perform the exercises that produced that body, and I am reminded of the profession I was forced to give up, it's easy to weep. I am weeping for the former Temple, my former life of health, career, pain free existence, and perceived freedom. However, when I am reminded of how last year I battled chronic illness that made it impossible for me to even leave the house, and look at the foundation of this year, where I am able to attend church, go out to dinner with my husband here and there, I shout His praises on the rooftops, worshiping Him for the restoration He is bringing me incrementally. Even the near death experience before Christmas doesn't stop the praise, because I am learning to lay my foundation for this new Temple, this new season in worship, praise and JOY. It doesn't matter that instead of a courtyard surrounding this new Temple there are ruins. The ruins will be dealt with. In fact, the ruins were dealt with in Nehemiah, the book after Ezra. Ah, but the Temple, the Temple is the spiritual foundation which must be laid first. The wall represents protection against the Enemy, and let me say that while you are rebuilding your Temple, the Lord will protect you for you are laying down the foundation for the most important aspect of your life, His Kingdom.

If the priests and leaders could, I am sure they would love to take the wisdom they gained while in exile and combine it with the beauty and glory of the old Temple. I would love to do that too, wouldn't you? But it doesn't work that way, and we must remember Isaiah 43:19, "See, I am doing a new thing! Now it springs up; do you not perceive it? I am making a way in the wilderness and streams in the wasteland." His Word does not say, " I am combining some of the old and some of the new". Our desire to cherry pick the pieces of our journey and mold them together somehow doesn't work. In fact, the way that we find joy in our return to restoration, is to be grateful for the foundation of the new thing He is springing forth in our lives. We must perceive it. Perceive means to "recognize, discern, envision, or understand". It's okay to remember the former Temple, but let's not stay there. Instead, let us rejoice in the return to restoration.

Prayer Starter: Lord, thank you for the seasons of our lives, even the seasons that grieved us. Lord, help us perceive the new thing that You are doing in our lives. Help us see the foundation even if it's surrounded by ruins. We give You all of our rubble, Lord, all of the broken pieces around us, and we place them in the palm of Your Loving hand. We trust, You, Lord. Thank You for the new thing You are doing, Lord. Give us a discerning Spirit to see the truth on our journey to restoration. In Your Name we pray, Amen.

Growing Your Garden

"I am the true grapevine, and my Father is the gardener. He cuts off every branch of mine that doesn't produce fruit, and he prunes the branches that do bear fruit so they will produce even more. You have already been pruned and purified by the message I have given you.Remain in me, and I will remain in you. For a branch cannot produce fruit if it is severed from the vine, and you cannot be fruitful unless you remain in me." John 15: 1-4

When I think of gardens, I tend to think of beautiful places with abundant flowers and amazing colors. It's an oasis of sorts, a place where you can go and smell the sweet scent of beauty. True art from the master gardener right in front of us accessible to us.

Gardens to me are a place where we simply cannot doubt the hand of God. But the thing about Gardens is they don't happen by accident.

Gardens are intentional from the picking of the seed to the season where it must be planted everything about a garden is mapped out and planned from the soil to the seed to the flower. I'm not much of a gardener but recently in the last month, or so Holy Spirit has been inspiring me to plant some flowers. I don't have a lot of flowers, perhaps six or seven in the border of our front yard for aesthetic appeal. Honestly, any plant or flower I have ever owned has died. My ignorance on how to care for them and forgetting to water them really didn't help matters much. However, God was asking me to do this, and I wanted to do it right. I actually had to YouTube a video on how to plant a flower! That's how out of my comfort zone I was. The initial planting was a little tough. I had to dig out the rocks, and on our property, we have rocky soil. I had to dig them out one by one and create a place to be able to plant the flowers. I did not start from seed I admit; I picked up some young flowers that were beginning to sprout. I bought the correct soil and plant food, as well as a watering can. My flowers began to blossom, and I felt so proud that I had finally remembered to water them daily. Then they started dying, and I realized that watering them wasn't enough. I felt like a failure as I watched them wither away and I was helpless to stop it. I asked God, "Why would you have me plant these flowers if they were just going to die on my watch?" He said," It's true that you've watered them, and now they have grown but they have overgrown, and you have not pruned them."

Pruning? It looked like I was going to need to watch another YouTube video. I was always uncomfortable with the idea of pruning flowers. It felt like pruning was painful for them and I didn't know what I was doing and insecure about what to cut. I guess I thought if I avoided it completely the things that were dead would

43

just fall off. While in some cases that was true too much of what was dead stayed on the flower stunting its growth. Back to the store, I went purchasing pruning tools. I began to snip the back and cut the things that were not producing. I felt very insecure in the process. In fact, there was even a time when it looked like I did more harm than good because nothing was growing, and all I saw was a bunch of green! Still, I watered the flowers talking to them and speaking life to them. The next day I saw so much growth I was amazed. New blooms were sprouting up everywhere and what looked like a once dead flower looked brand-new! I was so excited! Then I noticed the flower starting to struggle again and I went back to God and asked Him why after watering and pruning the flowers were dying again? He said, "You have not taken into consideration the weeds growing around the flowers choking out its roots." So I began to weed the garden making sure that the flowers were protected and safe from the choking. I even noted how some weeds almost looked identical to the flowering plants. They tried to blend in so I would not notice. Again God pointed them out to me.

The three things that I found were most important in maintaining my little garden were: Pour, prune and protect. The flowers needed water and food, they needed to be pruned so they could grow to maximum potential and they needed protection from the weeds that sought to choke out their tender roots.I shouldn't have been surprised that God had me grow a garden right when we are in our season of releasing and grief. The last thing I wanted to do was grow a little flower garden. All I wanted to do was keep the five babies I grew and grow them more. I found it to be a poor replacement until I realized that it was not meant to replace anything at all. It was meant to teach me the importance of how to protect what He has grown in me. So many things can take away from our garden, but here are the ones I feel led to share.

1.Busyness- When we fail to drink at the well and feast at His table we are starving our Spirit, and that includes all of our growth He has cultivated within us as well. Yes, Jesus will water us, but we must be in His presence for that to occur. In our fast-paced lifestyle we cannot be watered if we are constantly moving. Just as the flowers soak up the nutrients from the soil, water, and food we too must be rooted in place to receive the spiritual food God has for us. Don't forget to water yourself by being intentional to take time to Worship, Read the Word, and Pray.

2.An Unteachable Spirit- We tend to think the fuller we are in knowledge the more spiritual we are. Just as a flower can be full of leaves and buds but not thrive, we too can be full of things that hold no benefit to us spiritually. If we do not allow God to cut the things that are a hindrance to us we will just keep growing wild. One of my flowers, in particular, did not have many dead leaves or buds but in fact was growing so much it was crowding out the other flowers causing them to perish. When I looked at its growth closer, I saw that letting it grow wild actually was crowding out some fresh buds that wanted to grow underneath the mess. From the outside, it looked like it was healthy, but a closer look showed it was growing wild and needed to be pruned. After pruning it, even more, buds arrived but grew with a purpose in the way I had pruned it. It did not crowd out the other flowers but rather added to the beauty of what was there. A person with an unteachable spirit feels that everything they say and do is fruitful when in reality it harms themselves and those around them. Letting God prune the things that don't bear much fruit allows a branch to grow that bears abundant fruit. Having a teachable spirit means we can ask God to search our hearts and reveal anything He wants to extract. It also means allowing ourselves to be convicted.

3. Roots of Bitterness/Unforgiveness- Those weeds though... Can I get an Amen? Seriously, I despise weeds. I will weed that little flower garden and create a border around it, and as soon as I turn around they are back with a vengeance! Why do weeds grow so fast? It's because weeds actually thrive and adapt in a disturbed habitat, such as a fallen tree from a storm. Guess what? Gardening is considered a disturbed habitat. This means that the tilling of the soil, planting of the seed or young flower actually creates an environment for weeds to come. It signals the weeds like a flare gun, "Hey I'm here." Even when weeds are pulled because their seeds do not germinate all at once, they keep returning. This is the same spiritually as well. We have spiritual weeds that ruin our Godly Garden. In fairness, the disturbance we create in the supernatural soil of our hearts when we accept Christ and let Him be our Master Gardener also sends out a flare gun response to the Enemy. So the Enemy begins to activate the seeds he planted in our hearts long ago, and because the memories and the bitterness and unforgiveness doesn't happen all at once, it seems that as you work through one layer of bitterness or unforgiveness, another layer appears. It can be an exhausting process especially when you see the weeds come back.

Romans 12:2 tells us, " Do not conform to the pattern of this world, but be transformed by the renewing of your mind. Then you will be able to test and approve what God's will is--his good, pleasing and perfect will." Renewal is not a one-time process but a continuous one, just as weeding is not a one and done process either but one that must be done on a regular basis. The truth is if you have a garden you will have weeds. When we ignore that fact or somehow think that our Gardens will be weed proof we disillusion ourselves. We must look at the weeds, identify them for what they are and then pull them out. We will be offended at times, we will get hurt, and we will have to forgive. There are layers to all of this as some wounds are so deep it cannot be pulled by hand, but it takes an inner healing to do it. Either way, we are responsible for the condition of our garden and part of the work is the process of continuous renewal of our minds. Ephesians 4:23 tells us, "Instead, let the Spirit renew your thoughts and attitudes".

Growing a garden is not an easy task, and it requires continuous work just like our spiritual walk. It requires drinking at the well of His Spirit, so we are not thirsty and allowing ourselves the painful process of being pruned by the Master Gardener. It also challenges us to protect the work God has done in us by guarding our hearts and not letting the enemy's weeds take root in our soil. How is your garden looking these days? What do you feel the Holy Spirit is leading you to do in caring for your garden?

Prayer Starter: Lord, I am not a very good gardener I admit, but You are. I submit myself to Your pruning while also committing myself to drink from Your well soaking in Your presence. Help me to renew my mind and guard my heart against the weeds that the Enemy is trying to use to choke out what You have planted. I trust You, Lord. Search my heart and reveal what needs to be uprooted. In Jesus Name, Amen.

Grief in the Garden

"There is a hidden spring called En Hakkore. It is a spring reserved for those who cry. If tears have streaked your face, and grief torn your heart, there is a spring of restoration that God has for you. Drink of this spring and be restored." Passion Translation Judges 15:19

Judges 15:19 "Samson's spirit was revived as he drank from the spring. So he named it En Hakkore -- "the spring for the one who cried."

The Lord knows the pain of every heart, even yours. He is not a distant spectator, but an intimate Father who sees and knows every moving of your heart, every disappointment of your life. In our first devotional in the Garden Series, we discussed ways to care for your spiritual garden as well as ways to remove the things that stunt the growth of the garden. Even though we may care for our garden well, it doesn't mean we won't experience grief. Life and death occur in gardens regardless of how well we may care for our bounty. Recently, a storm rocked my little garden. Buds were everywhere, and it seemed that nothing would grow again. One of my flowers, in particular, my favorite, had the heads come off. I had to cut them down, and all that was seen was the pruned stem. I was sad not realizing that more buds would bloom again because the root system was intact. A few days later these tiny little flower heads were curled under and began rising. Six beautiful bright flowers emerged a week or so later even fuller and more beautiful than before. Not having any gardening experience I thought of the ebb and flow of maintaining a garden one of which is to accept the life cycle and death cycle of what is planted.

Dry seasons where there is no rain can be hard on gardens in the natural and spiritual realm. We all have gone through those desert seasons. Weary and knowing what we have to face we are dreading what lies ahead. It's too painful, and we cannot seem to breathe much less drink. In Judges 15, Samson made a mess by falling in love with a pagan woman and marrying her. After being denied her, he took revenge on the Philistines. Although Samson made the mistake of marrying a Philistine woman and bringing trouble for his people, God used the circumstances to destroy Israel's enemy. After destroying one thousand Philistines with a jaw bone of a donkey, he cried out to the Lord for water and the Lord gave it to him. Samson's strength and body became revived. The irony of grief is that it produces water through tears yet parches the soul. The act of pouring out sorrow is draining and is felt physically as well as spiritually. I've been there in those places where my body was producing so many tears, but my intake was low. It felt like anything that was poured in just came right back out again. Sustaining your garden during grief is hard. Isaiah 51:3 says, "The Lord will comfort Israel again and have pity on her ruins. Her desert will blossom like Eden, her barren wilderness like the garden of the Lord. Joy and gladness will be found there. Songs of thanksgiving will fill the air." Grief in the garden can make you feel that nothing will grow again.

Jesus understood grief quite well and in fact, when facing the crucifixion, prayed in the Garden of Gethsemane, which means Olive Press. Here, in this place of grief, anticipating betrayal of spiritual brothers and torture, Jesus was pressed. He was in such grief that He actually sweated blood. Much was pouring out of Jesus in those moments as He asked His Father if there was any other way. No intercession was happening as His disciples could not even stay awake to pray for their beloved friend and Rabbi. The Garden of Gethsemane was host to Olive trees. Olive trees are virtually indestructible and can grow in any soil, flourish in great heat and with very little water. Oh, to be an Olive Tree in those moments of grief. Even when an Olive tree is cut down new life will grow back from its roots. The Olive tree is a lesson on perseverance and endurance. Interestingly enough the Olive tree has also been a symbol of peace in Israel and here was Jesus, the Prince of Peace, being pressed to persevere in the garden of grief. As Jesus, prepared for death there are a few things we can learn from Jesus while in the Garden of Grief:

1. **Jesus asked for intercession from His inner circle-** "Then Jesus went with them to the olive grove called Gethsemane,

and he said, 'Sit here while I go over there to pray.' He took Peter and Zebedee's two sons, James and John, and he became anguished and distressed. He told them, 'My soul is crushed with grief to the point of death. Stay here and keep watch with me.'" Matthew 26:36-38. Grief is isolating in that it makes you feel as if you are cut off from the rest of life. I remember after my daughter Eve passed, I would go food shopping and see people laughing and living. It seemed as if my life had stopped, but everyone else's kept going. It's those moments when it's tempting to believe that no one could understand what you are going through. Friends wanted to meet with me and talk with me, but I had nothing to share. I just wanted to curl up into a ball, but with my newborn son, there was no time for any of it. People would tell me how happy I must be to have a newborn son, but all I could think of was his twin Eve, who I didn't have. Other times people would tell me that "at least I had Christian" as if he was a consolation prize. Yes, grief is a place that is so tender it seems just easier to avoid the clumsiness of others completely. When we look at Jesus, the most misunderstood man on the planet, we see that although He knew He would be let down, He still asked His inner circle to intercede. He still reached out. He expressed disappointment too when they all fell asleep during His turmoil. When you are being pressed, it's important to reach out to your inner circle, a safe place to share. The disciples didn't understand the magnitude of Jesus's grief, nor did they even understand what was about to take place. Just like no one understood that taking there is no "at least" when your son's twin dies. There is no "at least" when you are going through a grief period.

2. **Jesus accepted Father God's decision-** "He went on a little farther and bowed with his face to the ground, praying, "My

Father! If it is possible, let this cup of suffering be taken away from me. Yet I want your will to be done, not mine." Matthew 26:39 When we are facing grief do we accept the decision of God our Father? I struggled with this. TIme after time I heard testimony after testimony of healing that took place in babies. I wondered "Why not my Eve"? It was difficult to fathom that God would allow Eve to die but save other children. This was where I was challenged because the truth is if I believed God is good all the time then can I say He is good even though He allowed our family to suffer so much? The answer is yes. Circumstances change but God never changes, and if we treat this as the absolute truth that it is we, like the Olive tree, will be able to grow strong again even if chopped down by tragedy. Knowing why will not change your circumstances. It doesn't matter. Loss is loss, and it still hurts. Jesus could have made so many other choices other than enduring the cross. He could have utilized His power and authority given to Him by the Father. He could have questioned the goodness of His Father. He did no such thing. Instead, Jesus ended His prayer with "Thy will be done." Submitting to God's will no matter how painful is the only way to heal. Grief if left to fester will try and convince you that God is not good, resulting in roots of bitterness. I have seen the hardened hearts of those weathered by grief, and I have also seen fear take root as well. For me, grief that I had held in resulted in fear. I stayed up all night after taking Christian home from the hospital days after losing Eve. I wondered if he was breathing? What if he dies too? How can I protect him when I could protect Eve? Do you see how that works? The Bible says that there may be tears in the night, but joy comes in the morning. How is that possible that grief and joy can coexist? Pure grief, given to the Father in trust will heal. It will even create a spiritual strength and enduring roots like the Olive tree. Grief handled our way will ruin our

Garden until nothing new will grow, and all that was there choked out by fear and bitterness.

3. **Jesus still ministered:** "But Jesus answered, "No more of this!" And he touched the man's ear and healed him." Luke 22:51. When the soldiers came to arrest Jesus, one of the disciples cut off a soldier's ear. Jesus immediately put a stop to the violence and healed the man's ear. Can you imagine? Here are the soldiers who will play a major part in the torture of Jesus, and He heals one? Grief convinces us that we are too traumatized to be of any use. While I agree that there is a healing time necessary for self-care to take place, my testimony of trusting God through Eve's death became a way to witness to people about the goodness of God. People saw faith, perseverance, and endurance in my story and it encouraged them that they too can be victorious rather than staying a victim. Sharing Jesus has always been a part of who I am. That didn't change because Eve died. In fact, letting God use it for His glory brought more healing than I could have ever imagined. Jesus healing the man's ear was just who He was. Jesus was a prophet and a healer as well as a teacher. Even in the midst of chaos, betrayal, and grief, He ministered to the soldier. While before the council, Jesus did not deny who He was even though it meant death on the cross. Grief can cause us to lose our identity if we are stagnant. It is important to remain in Him as Jesus remained in His Father. Jesus gave His life for us, are we willing to give our grief to Him?

Isaiah 40:29 tells us that "He gives power to the weak and strength to the powerless." We can rely on His strength as we find safe places to share our grief. Even in our weakened state, we can minister because of His power and strength flowing through our veins. We are not alone in the Garden of Grief, much can and will grow there if we follow the principles of Jesus.

Prayer Starter: Lord, I am taking inventory right now of this garden, and all I see are tears. Tears can grow the seed buried in sorrow if I just release it all to You. Take me deeper in You, Lord, deeper into Healing, even though it hurts, even though I am weary and just can't take another hit. You are my fortress, my strength, and my shield, and I declare and decree that I can do ALL things through Christ who strengthens me. Thank You Lord for your mercy and your unfailing Love, In Your Name, I pray, Amen.

Gaining Ground in the Garden

"At the place where Jesus was crucified, there was a garden, and in the garden a new tomb, in which no one had ever been laid." John 19:41

We have discussed in our Garden Series how to grow our garden and how to handle grief in the garden. We saw how Jesus handled grief knowing the agony of what He was about to endure. Jesus was crucified on Calvary's cross in a place also known as Golgotha; both names mean skull. Some scholars say it was because the mountain looked like a skull. Others argue it was because it was where most crucifixions took place for several reasons. The Romans used this place to warn criminals that no crime would be tolerated. It's location right outside of the city gates was a prime location to make a statement. However, the Jews also had strict laws about dead bodies' proximity to the living. So this location seemed to work for all involved, but most importantly it sends a more important message to us. Golgotha was a garden. How is it possible that a place that means skull and is where crucifixions took place mean garden? How can a place where Jesus gave Himself to the cross be a garden? What can possibly grow there? In fact, where Jesus is buried is known as the "garden tomb." John 19:41 says, At the place where Jesus was crucified, there was a garden, and in the garden a new tomb, in which no one had ever been laid."

It's not a coincidence that Jesus experienced His greatest victory in a garden while Adam experienced his greatest failure in the Garden of Eden. Paul said in 1 Corinthians 15:45, "The Scriptures tell us, 'The first man, Adam, became a living person.'But the last Adam—that is, Christ—is a life-giving Spirit." The name Eden means "delight" and in Aramaic means "fruitful and well-watered." Adam and Eve were given the gift of immortality and fellowship with the Great I Am, but their sin poisoned the environment, closing it off to mankind forever. Jesus died in a Garden that meant "skull" where the bones of other criminals were carelessly discarded. Tortured and crucified He hung on a cross and the blood that He shed poured over the garden of Golgotha in Calvary watering it spiritually bringing life. Jesus, in the very place of death bought us back, paid for us to be free and won the greatest war ever fought: the war for our souls.

When we look at how Jesus died, it's hard to look at it as victory. Our flesh cringes at the thought of our Jesus suffering. It's safer to imagine Him resurrected, but lest we forget as the disciples might have, He bares the scars. More importantly, Jesus shows us how to attain victory when we are in that place of suffering as well as what to expect right before our divine destiny. Jesus moved from the grief of Gethsemane into the very destiny that would bring Him victory. Still, the cross was the way, the only way, to attain that victory. There are certain things the enemy likes to throw at us when we are close to our destiny.

1.**Expect False Accusations**- Right before we enter our divine destiny, we can expect to endure false accusations. There are those who simply do not want to see the manifestation of all that God has for you in your life. They do not want to see you grow and so instead they will use gossip, false accusations and the like to slander you. The key is to handle it like Jesus.

"The chief priests and the whole Sanhedrin were looking for evidence against Jesus so that they could put him to death, but they did not find any.Many testified falsely against him, but their statements did not agree.Then some stood up and gave this false testimony against him: "We heard him say, 'I will destroy this temple made with human hands and in three days will build another, not made with hands.' " Yet even then their testimony did not agree.Then the high priest stood up before them and asked Jesus, "Are you not going to answer? What is this testimony that these men are bringing against you?"But Jesus remained silent and gave no answer". Mark 14:55-61

The chief priests were so hungry for blood that they looked for something, anything to sentence Jesus to death. Finding nothing, they made up false testimony but could not even get their stories straight. It's important to note that Jesus did not respond to their false accusations, rather He let their own character be revealed in the situation. Their slander needed no defense. When in the same situation as we discussed in the devotional about offense, it is important to let God vindicate not you.

2. Expect Condemnation- Along with accusation comes punishment, and this is the nature of condemnation. It is a form of sentencing and many experience this right before their divine destiny takes hold. Punishment can be anything from being "ghosted" by church members, where everyone who you once spent time with disappears from your life suddenly, or even being publicly ostracized for your Faith. Either way, condemnation is usually connected to walking in your identity. When you walk in your Christ-given identity, call and purpose for your life unapologetically expect condemnation.

"Again the high priest asked him, "Are you the Messiah, the Son of the Blessed One?"
"I am," said Jesus. "And you will see the Son of Man sitting at the right hand of the Mighty One and coming on the clouds of heaven." The high priest tore his clothes. "Why do we need any more witnesses?" he asked. "You have heard the blasphemy. What do you think?"
They all condemned him as worthy of death. Then some began to spit at him; they blindfolded him, struck him with their fists, and said, "Prophesy!" And the guards took him and beat him." Mark 14:62

What made everyone so angry with Jesus? He uttered one sentence, and they had all they needed to condemn an innocent man. Jesus broke His silence only when His identity was questioned. He did not need to defend Himself against the accusations because they were baseless and Jesus knew His Father was the vindicator. When it came to His identity which was connected to His destiny, He stated the truth about who He was. The revelation of identity is what sparked the condemnation and brutal beating. Jesus handled the question about His identity truthfully. Despite any condemnation we may be facing, it is important that we are honest in revealing who we are in Christ and what we are called to do. Our mission given to us by God can not be thwarted by man. Had Jesus stayed silent, who knows what would have happened? We are not called to be intimidated or stay silent in the face of questioning even though it means suffering.

3.Expect Mockery- One you stand firm in your identity in Christ expect to be mocked for your beliefs and the call God has on your life.This is evident before any great move of God. It has happened to me in prophetic ministry before and is meant to make you question what you do and who you are. Don't let it. I have encountered many who call themselves Christians balk against the idea of prophets and prophecy and personally attack because of it. I did not respond to their accusations or mockery, but I did keep on operating in the gift God has given me as He has called me to do. I have experienced mockery because of my zeal for the Holy Spirit, but still, I did not stop pursuing God and basking in the glory of His Spirit.

"The soldiers led Jesus away into the palace (that is, the Praetorium) and called together the whole company of soldiers.They put a purple robe on him, then twisted together a crown of thorns and set it on him. And they began to call out to him, "Hail, king of the Jews!" Again and again, they struck him on the head with a staff and spit on him. Falling on their knees, they paid homage to him. And when they had mocked him, they took off the purple robe and put his own clothes on him. Then they led him out to crucify him." Mark 15: 16-20

Upon cruel physical and verbal mockery, Jesus did not recant or give up on who He was. He endured, and that is what we need to do as well. Jesus did not stay silent because He was weak. He stayed silent because He was strong. Most think strength comes from fighting back, but that is easy to do when attacked. True strength is submitting to God's plan and purpose even when you are relentlessly attacked. Jesus fighting back would not have benefitted the purpose God had for His life and the destiny that was before Him. In fact, doing so would have ruined it. With one snap of His finger, Jesus could have had warrior angels dismantle the attack. Think of the strength it took to allow Himself to be falsely accused, mocked and condemned when He had the power to stop it. Let's not forget that with one Word Jesus could have proved "He was right" wiping the smug looks off of the accuser's faces and releasing Himself of the agony. He did no such thing because His suffering was necessary to fulfill His purpose thereby launching Him into His destiny.

I want to be clear that I am not advocating in this devotional that people allow themselves to be emotionally, verbally or physically abused. If that is what you are gleaning, then you are missing the point. There is only one Jesus, and it was His destiny to die for our sins, and this was the only way to free us from the shackles we placed on ourselves in Eden through sin. The point is we are going to experience mockery, condemnation, and accusation in our Christian walk, but it's how we handle those things that show our maturity and readiness for the call.

Prayer Starter: Lord, I know I need Your strength to stand for You even when it hurts, especially when it hurts. Help me handle accusations, mockery, and condemnation with Your authority and with Your wisdom. Thank You, Lord, for Your sacrifice so I could live fully and completely in You. In Your Name, Amen.

Gaining Victory in the Garden

In Part three of our Garden Series, we discussed what to expect while in the throws of our wilderness season. Right before any great move of God regarding our destiny the Enemy attacks. We discussed several things to expect when you are just about to step into your destiny: accusations, condemnation, and mockery. Jesus endured all of this and much worse on the cross. There is one last thing Jesus endured right before committing His Spirit, conquering death and adopting us as His people. It is the very thing that creeps up on us subtly: Temptation. I don't know about you, but when I think of temptation, I think of a not so obvious sneaky person trying

61

to lure me into doing something I shouldn't. It's easy for us to believe that temptation is obvious because if we understood how subtle it really is, we might have to examine our lives a little more closely.

Temptation is not always an overtly bad thing. In fact sometimes it's not anything "bad" at all, which is how we can become trapped in the first place. Temptation is not always an Adam and Eve moment. It's not even a Jesus in the desert moment where He was tempted to turn stones to bread. No, unfortunately, temptation can be so much more subtle than that. When we are in a place of suffering right before our divine destiny, there will always be something offered to try and numb the pain. It can be anything that is used with the intent of escaping the pain of the prison. Whether it be emotionally, physically, spiritually or financially, whatever we use to distract us from our purpose is a detriment. Distraction is a form of Temptation as it attempts to get our eyes off of God and our purpose.

Jesus knew what it was like to deal with distraction. In Jesus's case, many are confused regarding the drink Jesus was offered while dying on the cross. Let's take a closer look.

Mark 15:23 states, "Then they offered him wine mixed with myrrh, but he did not take it."

Matthew 27:34 says, "they offered Him wine to drink, mixed with gall; but after tasting it, He refused to drink it."

When we look at Mark and Matthew, we see that the word "gall" means bitterness and so gall and myrrh were the same thing here indicating that the bitter substance mixed with wine was intended to anesthetize Jesus. Myrrh is a bitter substance known to alleviate pain. In Mark and Matthew, we see that Jesus was offered something to stupefy Him and numb the agony He was in. He refused.

John recalls the vinegar soaked in a sponge on the stalk of a Hyssop plant and Matthew recalls the second instance of a drink being offered. Luke mentions wine vinegar offered to mock.

John 19:28-30 says, "Later, knowing that everything had now been finished, and so that Scripture would be fulfilled, Jesus said, "I am thirsty." A jar of wine vinegar was there, so they soaked a sponge in it, put the sponge on a stalk of the hyssop plant, and lifted it to Jesus' lips. When he had received the drink, Jesus said, "It is finished." With that, he bowed his head and gave up his spirit.

Matthew 27:45-50 "From noon until three in the afternoon darkness came over all the land. About three in the afternoon Jesus cried out in a loud voice, "Eli, Eli ,clemasabachthani?" (which means "My God, my God, why have you forsaken me?")When some of those standing there heard this, they said, "He's calling Elijah."Immediately one of them ran and got a sponge. He filled it with wine vinegar, put it on a staff, and offered it to Jesus to drink. The rest said, "Now leave him alone. Let's see if Elijah comes to save him. Then Jesus shouted out again, and he released his spirit."

Luke 23:36 "The soldiers also came up and mocked him. They offered him wine vinega.r"

There are two things that are important to recognize. First, when Jesus was offered the anesthetic drink, He refused, knowing that He must endure the suffering rather than anesthetize it. The second time He was offered a drink it was vinegar with the Hyssop reed. The vinegar was not an act of mercy, and it contained no drug or anesthetic in it rather it was an act of mockery and torture. The purpose of it was to prolong the pain as it did not actually relieve thirst at all. It was intended to refresh just enough to lengthen the time frame of agony. In both cases where the vinegar was given with the Hyssop reed, Jesus breathed His last breath. The hyssop reed was also used in the Old Testament Exodus 12:22, as a paintbrush to apply the lamb's blood to the doorpost so the Angel of Death would pass. Once again this is no coincidence as Jesus, the sacrificial lamb was given a drink to mock and prolong death with the hyssop reed. He took the weight of our sins with His blood. Hyssop also represented cleansing as well as purification and Jesus in His death cleansed us with His blood shed for us. Now, we appear white as snow before Father God.

In Psalm 69:21 David says, "They also gave me gall for my food And for my thirst they gave me vinegar to drink." This is considered a Messianic prophecy applying metaphorically to David but literally to Christ. David felt like this in his Psalm, but Jesus actually endured it.

There are times in the throws of our own painful circumstances the Enemy will offer an anesthetic. It will be something to numb the pain and seemingly "help us" endure the circumstance. In reality, this is not something that will help at all, but render you unable to think clearly. Jesus could not be rendered unconscious or drugged. Part of His purpose was to bear the burden of sin on His shoulders. He needed clarity for such a task. Jesus doesn't offer us vinegar to drink when we come to Him thirsty. He offers us rivers of living water. That's the difference. Temporary fixes with the purpose of "helping us" only become idols later on. That which numbs the pain now will numb His Spirit later. It will take the place of God on the throne and become an idol. Whether it's alcohol, food, busyness, a spouse or our children, that which we dive into to avoid feeling pain will only prolong our pain. That which we dive into to avoid working on ourselves and going deeper will stagnate us. There are so many things that the Enemy can use as a temptation into the bondage of distraction. I can't tell you how many times I have used chores and tasks and busyness to avoid the pain of loss. Was my checklist wrong? Was cleaning my home and making dinner and such a bad thing? No. However, the intent behind it was wrong. The intent of my heart was to stay busy to avoid the pain of loss. I wasn't staying still because it hurt too much. When the Enemy can use something good to distract us, it prolongs the healing process. We wander around the same mountain over and over never reaching the top. It's hard to be in a place of pain, and harder to handle it without using something to dull the agony. The good news is that in the death of Jesus we were given a Comforter who can give us peace that surpasses all understanding. Believe me, I am proof that joy comes in the morning.

Jesus, in His death on the cross, shows us how to refuse that which attempts to alter our destiny by altering our mind and heart. Instead, Jesus drank the vinegar so we could drink from Living Water. In doing so, Jesus taught us of the value of endurance and perseverance in the most painful of circumstances. This is where victory was won. The place of death is where resurrection took place. When you are in that place of refinement before your destiny, it hurts because there are parts of you dying. In place of death to self, a new creature is formed. One with a renewed mind and renewed strength. Jesus borrowed the grave for three days and rose again, crushing the Enemy. The Garden of Golgotha was where Jesus died, but it was also where He rose again. Are you willing to die to self and rise again? I know it hurts, and Jesus knows your pain, but on the other side of that death is deliverance and destiny. What is keeping you distracted from your destiny today?

Prayer Starter: Jesus, this hurts, and I don't like this place of pain. Help me discern the subtle (or not so subtle) distractions in my life preventing me from my destiny. Search my heart, Lord, and reveal that which is keeping me from seeking you in this place. I don't want vinegar Lord, and I don't want the gall, those things will never satisfy me as You will. Lord, instead I want to drink from the fount of Your Living Waters, so I will never be thirsty again. I declare and decree that I will rise up on the wings of eagles, that I will run and not grow weary and that I will walk but not faint (Isaiah 40:31). I pray this in Jesus' Name, Amen

After prayer write the answers to these questions;

1.What has the Holy Spirit revealed as your distractions? Write it down

2.Ask Holy Spirit; Holy Spirit why am I giving in to the temptation of these distractions? What is the underlying reason? Write it down.

3.Repentance- Father forgive me for choosing _____ over You. I realize now that I am using _____ to avoid the pain of _____. I give you this situation and I place it into Your capable hands. I now receive Your perfect peace that surpasses all understanding. I am trusting You, Lord. Help me to guard my heart against distractions.

4. Choose scriptures to create declarations and decrees regarding your personal situation.

The Beauty of Broken

"But he was pierced for our transgressions,
he was crushed for our iniquities;
the punishment that brought us peace was on him,
and by his wounds we are healed." Isaiah 53:5

I remember staring at my postpartum body in disbelief. Perhaps it was the movies or the magazines at the time, but I honestly believed my body would "go back" to normal after my twins were born. Instead, I felt like gravity took hold, and the secret and beautiful spaces where life lived and grew for nine months protested the emptiness. I cried. I cried for the loss of what once was and what would never be again. I didn't look in the mirror and see something miraculous; I saw brokenness. I still had huge bruises from the IV site where a life-saving blood transfusion was given, the edema I thought would dissipate immediately hung on for a few more weeks. As I hobbled along wearing the flip flops that were the only things that fit my feet, to attend to my screaming baby, I felt the C-section stitches pull painfully. I looked at the staples, and at that moment I felt utterly alone, hopeless, and broken. My stomach wasn't the only thing hanging on by something piercing and painful; my soul was too. I felt the loss of Eve heavily in those moments, but especially, I felt the loss of myself. I felt shattered into a million pieces wondering how I would be put back together. My emotions were all over the place, as my husband went back to work, and the new disease birthed along with my twins raged on. Boxes of baby things laid all around, and I couldn't clean up. The doctor warned me to rest and not lift. I wanted to laugh. Rest? I am a new mother, lady! The organization that I needed for my environment to feel safe was gone. Broken. The hopes of Christian and Eve playing together? Broken. My body's ability to ever conceive again? Broken. I felt as if I gave birth to brokenness when in reality, brokenness gave birth to me.

During any birthing process ligaments shift, move and stretch as the whole body prepares for something new to arrive. It is no different in the spiritual realm as well. Jesus knew suffering, the most excruciating kind. He was tortured, wounded, scarred and "crushed," broken so that we can be whole. He was broken so that we could be free. Jesus' brokenness was an act of war, conquering Death, defeating the Enemy, and bringing eternal life to His people. In His death, Jesus birthed life. There is nothing beautiful about what happened to Jesus when we look at it from the natural lens. It was messy, excruciating, and undeserved. I cannot even watch the Passion, without wanting to open fire on my Savior's persecutors.

When I look at it from the human perspective, I am tempted to feel sorry for Jesus, viewing Him as a victim. Nothing can be further from the truth. In choosing death, Jesus chose life for us, and this makes Him a Victor, a Conqueror, and our Savior. This was a living sacrifice. His body paid the price for what He birthed in the natural and supernatural realm. His brokenness gave birth to freedom.

Birthing takes place when we break something valuable to us, shattering it for what we know is coming rather than what we see in the now.

"While he was in Bethany, reclining at the table in the home of Simon the Leper, a woman came with an alabaster jar of very expensive perfume, made of pure nard. She broke the jar and poured the perfume on his head." Mark 14:3

Spikenard was very expensive, and in fact was worth a year's wages. For the woman to pour the perfume on Jesus' head, she had to break the seal. In order for this woman to give Jesus the best of what she had, the seal had to be broken first. What has to break in us in order to give Jesus the best of who we are? This anointing of Jesus' body was in preparation for His death. Sometimes we feel we are wasting our years in our current circumstances. I have felt this way and still struggle when I look at how many years I have spent struggling with illness. In my moments of fear and sadness, I will cry over losing my thirties to illness. I mourn the freedom I had to go and do what I pleased, and I become angry at the cost of the revelation this illness has allowed me. I will count how many years I have left, and pray that they are not plagued with this disease. What if I changed my perspective? What if I looked at this period in my life as labor pains? What if I saw the stillness as a gift from above training me for my purpose? What if I break the seal of sorrow and pour all of me into this season of labor? What if I stay focused on pouring the thing that I value the most over the One who values me the most rather than looking at how empty the perfume bottle is becoming? The breaking of the seal, the jar, showed the woman's faith in what was about to happen. While the others rebuked her for "wasting" the perfume on Jesus, He saw it differently. He saw the purpose in the breaking, the meaning of it and the sacrifice. He saw the sacrifice in the now as preparation for the future.

"My sacrifice, O God, is a broken spirit; a broken and contrite heart you, God, will not despise." Psalm 51:17

When we come to God with our brokenness, we are open to instruction. There is humility and earnestness in the unmaking of what we are and who we thought we would be. There is a shift in perspective, and tenderness by which we are nurtured and cared for. This is true even today when we face the shattering of our dreams in the now; we can be assured that the sacrifice of handing them over holds purpose. The shattering and the breaking are the labor pains of what is to come forth. It's the death of a season for a new harvest. It is allowing the tears of today to water the seed of tomorrow. This is the beauty of broken.

Prayer Starter: Father, I come to You in all of my brokenness. I need Your help in this season of labor as the intensity of the battle increases. Teach me and nurture me in this season, Lord. Let me feel Your presence and focus on the beauty in the breaking. Fill the cracks and spaces with all of You, for I know You will not leave me or forsake me. I thank You, Lord, for making beauty from ashes, using all of my afflictions as preparation for the future You hold in the palm of Your Mighty Hand. In Your Name, Amen.

The Story of Scars

"Look at my hands and my feet. It is I myself! Touch me and see; a ghost does not have flesh and bones, as you see I have." Luke 24:39

I was close to eleven years old and innocently swirling around the kitchen in my school uniform while chatting with my mother who was preparing dinner. She warned me that she had boiling water and pasta she was draining. I was in my own world and lost my

71

balance while twirling and bumped right into her, and the boiling water spilled onto my arm. I remember I was wearing a blouse and a sweater, so it took a second for the burning pain to sear me, but when it did, I was undone. I screamed louder than I ever had and my father ran up the steps of our home two at a time calmly taking me to the bathroom to roll up my sleeves and run the burn under cold water. We had just moved upstate from Westchester and did not know our way around. We drove around for an hour looking for the hospital while my arm was hanging out the window to stay cool. Nothing but cold could make that burning sensation go away. In the emergency room, they put constant cold packs on it and then ointment and finally a cast. I had second and third-degree burns over my arm and part of my dominant hand. I couldn't sleep, and I was in constant pain. Finally, the cast came off, and more draining of blisters and painful cleanup had to be done. My arm was raw and red and hurt to the touch. Over the next several years, people who saw the scar asked me what happened. I had to tell the story over and over again. At first, it was difficult to tell the story. I was embarrassed at my clumsiness and petrified of getting burned again. I would not even assist my mother in the kitchen when pasta was made. Boiling water and I had an understanding that we would not meet again. The scars reminded me of that quite well. Through God's grace, my hand has no scar, as it dissipated over the decades. Little did I know that my burn was not the only scar I would receive walking this journey called life. Other scars would emerge both physical, emotional and spiritual, and I would be called to share those stories as well. That's the thing about scars; they come from circumstances we would just as soon forget, but leave a mark ensuring that we never will.

In our first devotional called, "The Beauty of Broken" we discussed how God uses brokenness to birth something new within us. The labor pains of broken gives way to a new season of purpose and provision. But what about the scars? Why do they get to stay? After

Jesus died on the cross, His body broken to birth freedom, He was buried borrowing a grave for three days. He did not stay there. He rose again, conquered Death and then came to see His friends. He wanted to show them that what was prophesied had been true. I often wondered why Jesus still had His scars? When I was little, I remember pondering the reason. He just beat Death, surely He could have those removed, right? Now, I see the reason why Jesus kept those scars. Those scars told His story. Where there were wounds, no wounds existed any longer. Instead, the scars told the story of what happened, and they were the evidence needed to convince the disciples of who He was, and what He endured. In Luke 24:39, Jesus encouraged the disciples who thought He was a ghost, to handle Him. He said, "Touch me and see" rather than just, "Look". They were encouraged to examine His scars even to the point of touching them to know that Jesus was who He said He was. Jesus and His scars were proof of His identity. We were purchased at a cost, and the scars were the currency. We need to remember that while Jesus' scars allowed the disciples to identify Him, our scars do not define who we are.

Scars Remind Us of the Wounds He Has Healed

"He heals the brokenhearted and binds up their wounds." Psalm 147:3

"The righteous cry out, and the Lord hears them;
he delivers them from all their troubles.
The Lord is close to the brokenhearted
and saves those who are crushed in spirit.
The righteous person may have many troubles,
but the Lord delivers him from them all;
he protects all his bones,
not one of them will be broken." Psalm 34:17-20

Whether the wounds are physical or emotional, the scars that we take with us from those wounds remind us that a healing has occurred. Think about how beneficial this is for the future. Woundedness is a part of life, and the Bible tells us that the righteous have many troubles. When we find ourselves afflicted with a wound, we can look at our previous scars to remind us of the work He has already done. In the "Beauty of Broken" devotional, I mentioned that my childbirth wound made me feel broken and barely held together literally as well as figuratively. Now, when I see the scar, I see how far the Lord has taken me on this journey through grief and unspeakable joy. When I see bruised skin from the recent bout of illness that left me with angry IV marks, I remember that I serve one who "protects my bones." He keeps me whole. No matter what we endure, the scars remind us that He has healed us before and will do it again. He will keep us whole even when we feel broken.

Scars are a Testimony for Others

"He himself bore our sins" in his body on the cross, so that we might die to sins and live for righteousness; "by his wounds you have been healed."1 Peter 2:24

Our scars are a testimony for others. I want to be clear on this because our scars are not WHO we are, but show us WHO we serve. While Jesus used HIs scars to convince the disciples that He was truly alive, we are to use our identity in Him to show whose we are. Our scars must give glory to God, the one who heals our wounds because He was wounded. When we identify more with the scars than with our Savior, we can easily fall into a victim mindset. This mindset can turn into a stronghold as we show all of our scars evoking pity for our plight rather than honoring God as the key to our victory. When I share my story with others, it is not because I want people to see me as a victim but as a victor. My testimony is that despite the loss of our daughter, life-threatening illness, and financial crisis, we made it through because of who our God is. We chose faith, but it is He who was faithful. We were left with ashes, but it is He who has given us beauty. My scars say if we could get through these things in Christ then so can you! It's nothing that we have done, but it's what He is doing. He is the source of the healing. Yes, we are left with the scars, but it is so we may show others how He has worked in our lives.

We all have scars from various afflictions we have endured. Scars that are used for His glory come with a measure of authority. I can speak with authority on the grief of losing a child and chronic illness. I can speak with authority on raising a special needs child. I can speak with authority on maintaining intimacy and love in your marriage when faced with tragedy. Authority that comes from tragedy is a special gift given by God to reach others. Such authority does not count age as experience like traditional authority does, for it is so much deeper than that. This type of authority is an anointed authority. I encourage you today to let the Master Healer bind up your wounds. I encourage you to stop staring at your scars using them as your identity. Instead, ask God how He wants to use them. Let us say, "From now on, let no one cause me trouble, for I bear on my body the marks of Jesus."(Galatians 6:17). Let His healing tell the story of scars.

Prayer Starter: Father, I come to You today thanking You for my scars. Those wounds hurt, Lord, but I want to focus on the story of my scar. Show me how You want to use what the Enemy intended for evil for good, Lord. Show me how to reach others so that You may be glorified, Lord. Let my life be a sacrifice to You, the binder of my wounds, the Lover of my soul, the Keeper of my heart. You collect each tear, Lord, and I know you are using them to water the seed planted deep within my Spirit. Guide and direct me, and use my story for your glory. In Jesus' Precious and Holy Name, Amen.

The Scent of a Season

**"For I am about to do something new.
See, I have already begun! Do you not see it?
I will make a pathway through the wilderness.
I will create rivers in the dry wasteland." Isaiah 43:19**

When I was a little girl, I loved coming home. Aromas greeted me as I walked through the door depending on which season it was. Winter time was my favorite because there were always cookies baking, dough being made for pizza and meatballs frying in the pan. When snow storms were predicted my entire family, who lived within walking distance, would walk to our apartment with their sleeping bags. I remember the excitement knowing that there would be no formal bedtime and the cooking would commence. Laughter, food, and fellowship radiated from that little apartment. Cousins, Aunts, Uncles would tell stories, while the snow was gently falling or a blizzard raging. The next day, we would eat a large breakfast and spend more time together while my cousins and I would build snowmen and igloos on the small patch of grass we called a lawn. Hot cocoa awaited us when we came back in with red cheeks and noses. We didn't have much, but we had each other. The other day, Christian came home from school and while walking through the door, he inhaled deeply with his eyes closed and said, "Mama, everything smells so wonderful." I knew what he meant. A simple scent can take us back to the best moment of our lives and sometimes the worst. Tears filled my eyes as I willed his nose to remember this moment, because someday in the angst of being a teenager or the rush of becoming an adult he might forget to savor the scent. Our bodies were designed to feel the scent of a season in the natural environment. However, if we are still enough, we can discern the scent of a season in the supernatural realm as well.

Earlier in this series, we discussed the beauty of broken. God can take what we believe will shatter us, and use it to heal us instead. Brokenness humbles us and allows us to submit to the work that God wants to do in our lives. It's not that God causes the tragedies that shatter, but rather that He uses our brokenness to bring us a deeper healing than we ever thought possible. When we are broken, we are still, and in the stillness, God moves. In the second part of the series, we talked about the story of scars. Each scar tells a story, but we must not wrap up our identity in our scars. We must focus on the testimony that each scar represents. Scars give spiritual authority when we use them for His glory, not our own victimhood. Understanding both of these concepts is integral to recognizing when the season shifts. If we are wrapped up in our wounds and scars, then we are wrapped up in the past. The past loves to hold us prisoner, so we won't meet what God has for us in the present. God in His goodness wants to introduce us to what is next, but many times we remember the past, wrapped up in the memories and pain reliving each moment over and over again.

The first year after Eve's death was so incredibly painful because it was new. I smelled her cap that cradled her newborn head and just sobbed. The problem was that each year I was reliving the moment over and over again. Now, please understand that grief takes time. I am aware of that. Five years later, I still cry for my little girl, but it's different. Before, each year that passed by I was living as if the loss just happened. It was so fresh, and I wondered why it felt like it just happened even after two years went by, or three years went by. Was it always going to be like this? Yes, it would have been if I had not released my wound to God and let Him heal it. The truth was a lot had happened, and there was no time for grief. I hadn't allowed myself to share my tears and sorrow, not even with God. Once I handed it over to Him, let it out and shared my sorrow I began to find a deeper healing. God gently shared that this loss of mine became an idol, an identity, and an issue. My grief sat on the throne where God was meant to sit. At first, I was angry, but then I realized He was right. This was not living; this was existing. This was surviving not thriving. The tragedies we endure can easily become bondage that prevents us from catching on to the scent of a new season that God is leading us into. We cannot live in two time zones: the past and the present.

Isaiah the prophet spoke these words given to him by the Lord,

> **"For I am about to do something new.**
> **See, I have already begun! Do you not see it?**
> **I will make a pathway through the wilderness.**
> **I will create rivers in the dry wasteland." Isaiah 43:19**

He spoke of these new things as if they already happened, yet it was still unseen. The exiled people, the Israelites could not yet see it, as they were entrenched in the sufferings of the present in the wilderness. So occupied were they by their wounds in the wilderness, that they could not see the pathway of purpose God was creating in their midst. Although God moved mightily in the past for His people, it was forgotten, just as it is in our own lives. It's amazing how when tragedy strikes we immediately connect it to other tragedies that struck before looking at our circumstances as a pattern of strife in which we are the helpless victims. When God in His sovereignty delivers us from circumstances we immediately forget, and each time He delivers us it is as if He has never done so before. We are more comfortable connecting the strife from seasons past and seasons present as an offering of incense to Victimhood whom we have placed on the throne where God should be. So consumed are we with this incense that we cannot perceive this new thing. We cannot catch the scent of it; there is no vacancy. Where there is no vacancy, there is no filling, no perceiving, and hope dies a tragic death. As we are busy inhaling the scent of our sacrifice to other idols on our man made altar, what is being burned is the future, the new thing He has for us. Something must burn for the scent of the offering to placate our occupation with the past and the present suffering, and often it is the very thing that we were waiting for. How can we see it when all of our senses are focused elsewhere?

To catch the scent of a new season, you must first be aware of how God will use your present circumstances to move you into your new season even if your circumstances are less than favorable. The Israelites needed the comfort of knowing that God would create a way for them in their tumultuous journey through treacherous terrain. Our mindset must be one of opportunity. The more difficult the circumstances, the greater the work He will do. I find comfort in this thought when I am tempted to look at my past and present pain. This is not to say we do not cry or grieve. I am not suggesting that we pretend all is okay and avoid feeling the natural feelings of sadness or sorrow. I am simply reminding you not to STAY there. Second, it's also important not to despise the road that leads to a new season. Of course, a paved road is a much easier way to travel, but if you have rocks and weeds, then its intention is to refine you. Remember that your character has to match your new season. God is so efficient that He will even use the road you travel on to prepare you for this new adventure. Lastly, look at your own lane. I know it's hard and when we are struggling with our path, we tend to look at someone else's path, and it always looks better. What you are seeing is just a small chapter in their book, not the whole story. Focus on your own path and allow God to navigate that path for you. If your eyes are elsewhere, it will be easy to get lost.

When I am feeling attacked, I consider what is written about me in the books of heaven, and although I don't know it word for word, my Creator does. Our circumstances are merely a chapter in a larger book. They are not the whole story. Our purpose and destiny are so much bigger than that. A new season is upon you, do you not perceive it? He is ready to do a new thing in your life. Be patient, and stand strong. Can you smell the scent of a new season? It is fresh and new; it is destiny.

Prayer Starter: Father God, I thank You for the unique destiny You have for me. Prepare my heart for this new season and keep my eyes focused on You and only You. As painful as they are, I thank You for these circumstances that You are using to refine me, prepare me and propel me. I ask You for Your perfect peace to just cover me as I endure the terrain of this wilderness. Give me Your discerning Spirit so that I may realize the scent of a new season, and walk the road You have prepared for me. In Jesus' name, Amen.

Setting Up Your Season

"For everything there is a season,
a time for every activity under heaven.
A time to be born and a time to die.
A time to plant and a time to harvest.
A time to kill and a time to heal.
A time to tear down and a time to build up.
A time to cry and a time to laugh.
A time to grieve and a time to dance.
A time to scatter stones and a time to gather stones.
A time to embrace and a time to turn away.
A time to search and a time to quit searching.

81

A time to keep and a time to throw away.
A time to tear and a time to mend.
A time to be quiet and a time to speak.
A time to love and a time to hate.
A time for war and a time for peace."   Ecclesiastes 3:1-8

A while back I shared how God gave me a choice to shut down my business and wait on Him for my future or continue. I knew that He gave me Simply Eve Fragrances and in the season it helped with the healing I needed after losing Eve. Unfortunately, the timing is painful. Around this time in March five years ago, my husband Chris and I had the daunting task of cleaning out Eve's room. We took down the crib that we put up in Faith. We emptied the closet of her infant girl clothes, and took down the ladybug curtains and diaper table and her bedding. I remember the numb feeling as tiny little socks were put into a bin. This was death. This was worse than the sting of death because it was a false sense of calm before the storm. Downstairs Christian, my one month old stayed in my Mom's company while we cleaned things out. I heard his little cry for his bottle, and it felt that there was no space for me just to cry. Somehow life just went on when I felt like mine was in shambles. The needs of others were overwhelming, and I wished I could shut the door to Eve's room as I had done for the last month walking past it pretending it didn't exist; until it did. Those moments when Christian was newborn napping I would slowly climb the stairs and pause near Eve's bedroom door. I would open it a crack and peek in pretending that she was sleeping in there. I sometimes would walk in and hug the hangers of clothes or the ladybug pillow that came with the set. The room was cold, shut off from the heat source of the rest of the house, and it mirrored how I felt inside.

Fast forward to this week, when I am now overwhelmed by the task of dealing with my office which is in Eve's old bedroom. As I am shifting, and reorganizing I can't help but feel the death of something born out of sorrow. It feels so final, the legacy of Eve ending this way. I asked the Lord, "What will I use this bedroom for now?" In reality, I still make products for my family, and I do sell the muscle rub, bruise balm and wound balm that God said to keep. Still, so much material left, so much organizing to do, and I am so overwhelmed by the emotional work necessary for the task that I don't want to do anything at all. I find excuses to overclean the house, edit devotionals or write, and those things are fine on their own, but not as an excuse. Have you ever been there? Have you ever used busyness as an excuse so you wouldn't have to dig deeper into a healing that you know will hurt? I have, and in fact, I am doing it right now! The good news is that God wanted me to share this with you at this moment before I deal with the headquarters of Simply Eve Fragrances.

There have been so many words given to me by God about new seasons, and that is very exciting, but it's also hard. When a new season comes an old season ends, and many times we wrestle with what it looks like. Yes, Spring is coming, but Winter left its mark didn't it? And so the grounds need cleaning and tending to to prepare for what is to come. Many times I want to skip right over that hard stuff and just waltz my way into this new season. Anything seems better than being here, right? When we enter a grieving season, we become accustomed to it, even though it is painful, so when the season shifts and it is time to dance with joy we find we may have forgotten how. Our bodies are used to producing tears that our laughter feels a bit rusty. Just like the man or woman who goes to war and comes home to peace finds it difficult to acclimate to a civilian life so do we. The seasons in our lives help to shape us, but we also must understand that adjusting to a new season is not automatic.

Ecclesiastes shares with us that there is a time and a season for everything, but we must allow God to create the transition in our hearts to receive the season we are given even though we may not like it. In part three of our Destiny Series, The Scent of a Season we discussed that if we are unprepared for the new season, we can become disobedient, depressed, and destructive in our current season. Such is the case with Moses who was weary after wandering the desert for 40 years with the Israelites.

The Lord's Command

"Take the staff, and assemble the congregation, you and Aaron your brother, and tell the rock before their eyes to yield its water. So you shall bring water out of the rock for them and give drink to the congregation and their cattle." Numbers 20:8

Moses' Reaction

"And Moses took the staff from before the Lord, as he commanded him.

Moses Strikes the Rock

"Then Moses and Aaron gathered the assembly together before the rock, and he said to them, 'Hear now, you rebels: shall we bring water for you out of this rock?' And Moses lifted up his hand and struck the rock with his staff twice, and water came out abundantly, and the congregation drank, and their livestock." Numbers 20:9-11

The Consequences of Disobedience

"And the Lord said to Moses and Aaron, "Because you did not believe in me, to uphold me as holy in the eyes of the people of Israel, therefore you shall not bring this assembly into the land that I have given them." Numbers 20:12

From the outside looking in, it may seem a little harsh that ONE act would prevent Moses from entering the Promised Land, but if we look closely, we see that God judged the heart behind the action. The Lord gave Moses a command that would ensure He was upheld as Holy, that it was God doing all the work. When Moses struck the rock, he took matters into his hands making it appear as if he and Aaron were the miracle workers, not God. Even his wording implied pride "Shall WE bring water for you out of this rock?". Moses had become so used to this season, grabbing the staff parting the waters and other miracles that he was on autopilot. Between the desert heat, complaining Israelites, and broken commandments Moses couldn't help but feel, "Hey I didn't sign up for this." He didn't want it either, but this was his season, and he was transitioning from this season to the Promised Land, but his heart was compromised. Weariness had taken over and frustrated with the unbelief of the Israelites, Moses was disobedient in his response. He behaved as he had before driven by impulse and impatience rather than wisdom and obedience. He was supposed to speak to the rock, but he struck it instead. While we may sense the scent of a new season upon us let us be obedient in the one we are currently in. God calls us to speak to our current season not strike blows to it. The very season you are despising now is the refining tool that will allow your character to enter into this new season.

Setting up Your Season:

Walk in obedience- whatever God asks you to do, just do it. I know it's hard, believe me, there are so many times I feel as if I am walking in circles, but isn't that how the walls of Jericho fell? If you want your wall to fall, then you must obey.

Worship God in all circumstances- After the worship series in March, how can you not be prompted to lift your hands and praise

Him? This is a powerful weapon in getting your heart right for this new season.

Remember who you are and whose you are- When the season you are in is wearing on you and attacks are coming from all directions, remind yourself that you are a child of the King and you have access to His throne room. This is your identity. God chose you as a royal priesthood, and you are His Beloved. You belong to Him. Speak out scripture to remind yourself of identity.

Guard your heart- Moses had let frustration and bitterness enter his heart from the long and treacherous desert journey. While God gave Moses the staff to protect the people, Moses failed to guard the most important thing: his own heart. Each complaint out of the mouths of the Israelites was a planted seed. Moses was a prophet, and an intercessor, guarding his heart against bitter roots was integral.

Mind your mindset- The trip through the desert should only have taken ten days, but it took FORTY YEARS! The Israelites had heart issues from the mindset of victimhood. They were free but acted like slaves, even asking if they could return to Egypt because they would be fed good food there. So focused on what they were lacking they were unable to see the provision that God gave them in their desert season. Their constant complaining, unbelief, and straying from God delayed their new season by decades. When the Israelites were finally at the crossroads between the old season and the new, they became afraid. They did not believe that God would conquer the giants of the land. Even after all they saw, the Israelites did not have the "I serve a bigger God" mentality and so they wandered in the wilderness.

When Joshua was chosen to claim the new season of the Promised Land, it was with the heart of worship, obedience, and the humility of a vessel open to receive that God conquered. Once again, God arranged it so all would see His glory. This battle was not won with swords. I believe this is prophetic about our new season as well. We will not need to fight our way through in our own strength, or battle with human weapons. We simply need to guard our hearts and attitudes against mindsets that will leave us lingering in the desert longer. That being said, with a heart of obedience I will begin cleaning out the headquarters of Simply Eve Fragrances. I will do so knowing that it once was a room intended for my beautiful Eve, and the Lord changed it to a healing room where products were born to help people. Now, I'm not sure what the purpose of that room will be, my sight is blurry with the tears of this current season, but I know that He is setting up this new season, and I don't want to miss a thing.

Prayer Starter: Lord, this hurts. This season is full of tears. I don't want to cry, decisions I don't want to make and action when I want to be still. All of me is crying out for you to rescue me from this season, but I know Lord that You use everything to refine us for what is to come. Help me guard my heart against fear and discouragement and any mindsets that distract me from obedience. I trust You, Lord. You are a good Father, Lord. You love me, and I know that what hurts in this season will allow for joy in the next. Guide and direct my path to my Promised Land. In Your Holy Name, Amen

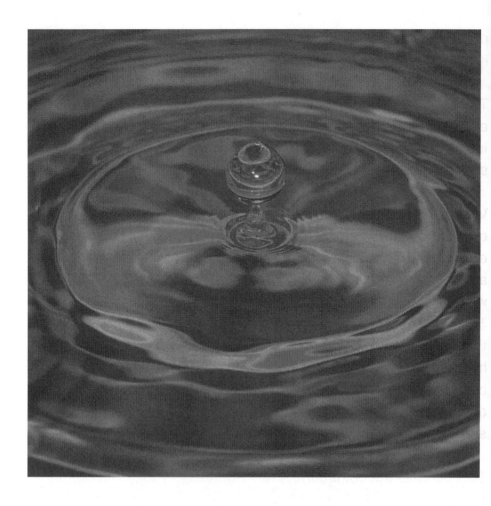

Viable Victory

"Jesus wept." John 11:32

How is it that five years ago today, I endured the most joyous and most tragic period in 24 hours? Today is the day that five years ago, I birthed two incredible children, Christian and Eve.

Sometimes when we think of victory, we think of the triumphant win. In our minds, the victor stands proudly with his sword held high and a smile on his face. However, we must change our mindset and instead imagine the victor bloodied from battle, weary to the bone, perhaps too tired to raise the heavy sword, but confident that he is indeed victorious because of Christ who strengthened him.

The definition of victory is "an act of defeating an opponent or enemy." In our case, the Devil is both. He both opposes Christ and is indeed set out to destroy us by any means possible. Does victory sound so glorious now?

Victory is not when everything's going right, but in fact is when everything is upside down in every way possible. We are bloodied, exhausted, and about to give up, but then we don't. We look above and say, "Lord, give me the strength to fight another day, for I am weary, and my flesh is failing. Please, Lord, I beg of you. Help me". THIS is victory. Every time we fight another day is victory. True, there are other times when immediate healings occur and miracles happen right before our eyes. These, too, are victories. However, the battles that are long, hard and challenging, the ones that make us question our faith, those battles are won when we choose to trust and love Christ despite them.

There comes the point during battles that are severe where we can choose to either turn towards Christ or turn away from Him. Losing my daughter was that battle. I remember the feeling of being robbed. God was supposed to heal my little girl, and it didn't happen. The news of a second autoimmune disease following felt like the final blow. I was incredibly angry. There I was, a funeral to plan, my colicky son to raise, and an auto-immune to survive. How could God allow this to happen to me? I often wondered. Sure, I yelled at Him and screamed and cried. Nobody seemed to understand that my son was not the consolation prize. I lost my daughter, his twin, but his life did not ease her loss.

After several weeks, I knew that I had a choice. Continue to be bitter and angry or turn towards Him. So, I turned towards Him. I said,

"Lord, I don't like you right now, but I love You. I still trust You even though this happened. I know that You are inherently good and that you are Sovereign. I know that Your ways are not my ways. While I don't understand what happened. I still know who You are, and I love You. I just do. Help heal me." This was a victory. From the outside people looked at our lives and saw victims of death, financial hardship, and illness, but that moment I felt victory. See, at that moment, I had a choice. I chose God, end of story. That moment, I won the fiercest battle of my life, the battle for my salvation. After experiencing all I had from God, I could not turn my back on Him. The Kingdom of Darkness lost that day, and every day since.

All battles come down to a choice. We must give ourselves time to grieve the loss of what we once held dear. Even Jesus wept throughout scripture for the beheading of John, and the loss of His friend Lazarus. No condolences or well-intended words would heal His pain. Jesus wept because He felt compassion. Jesus sweat blood over the thought of the agonizing pain He would endure on the cross. This did not mean Jesus was weak, but that He was human. However, let's look at the fact that despite the losses He experienced, He was victorious. He overcame Death, and because of this, we are now grafted to Him and within Him for eternity, as long as we accept Him.

Although this Christian walk is not an easy walk, victory does not look like it does in the movies we watch. Sometimes it boils down to a simple choice. What choice will you make when you are faced with battle? Just remember that grief is not a lack of faith and it is not defeat. It is part of living in this world where death lives too. Jesus wept, and Jesus grieved, it is a part of the journey, but it is not the destination. It is something I will remind myself of today, as I sing Happy Birthday to my son Christian, secretly hoping that God let's Eve hear it too.

My simple prayer for you today is that you would let the Master Healer touch those wounds with the Balm of Gilead. May you let the tears flow, like healing rain, because this is where the journey of healing begins.

"Grief"
There are certain wounds that even time cannot heal
The disquieting of the soul wells up as it struggles not to feel
Despite the passing time the heart still bleeds in pain
The tears that lose the fight swell and overflow falling like rain

The subconscious then betrays by giving dreams when asleep
The body feels the loss again as the conscious begins to weep
Only to awake and realize that it was a mirage nothing was true
You stand there being swallowed by grief and don't know what to do

Oh, Lord, I have beseeched You , "Please, no more grieving"
You've said that my Faith in You will sustain me, so it is this I am believing.
In Wisdom You have told me that it's a process I must endure
You sacrificed Your precious Son so we could live with you forevermore.

Each year someone tells me I am blessed to at least have one
A healthy boy who I adore, my miracle, and my son
What they don't understand that His life does not replace another
My little girl is not on earth to hug her parents or her brother

I cannot hold her or hug her and rock her to sleep
This kind of wound for a mother runs deep
"She is with Jesus! You will see her" they say
Yes, this is true, but does not comfort today.

Each holiday and birthday cuts like a knife
I think about death while I celebrate life
The painful bitter tags along marring the sweet
Knowing that your little family isn't complete

That there should be a little girl opening gifts on Christmas morn
She should blow out her candles with Christian on the day they
were born
She should run around playing with her little girl things
But God saw it fit instead to give her beautiful wings

So, Lord, until we get there would you please hold her tight?
Not sure when we will get there, but I know you have our flight
Until then we pray for peace that God gives as reprieve
And I thank you, Father, for the gift of our daughter, precious Eve.

Written by Nicole L. Cagna in Memory of Eve Luciana Cagna

Release to Receive

"Remember not the former things, nor consider the things of old. Behold, I am doing a new thing; now it springs forth, do you not perceive it? I will make a way in the wilderness and rivers in the desert." Isaiah 43:18-19

Recently, the Lord had put on my heart the Word, "Release to Receive". I understood the concept well. There were so many things in our lives that my husband Chris and I have had to release. In 2012 after God called us to the In Vitro process I gave birth to twins, Christian and Eve during an emergency C section where I nearly died from hemorrhaging losing half of the blood in my body. Eve was diagnosed with Trisomy 13 in utero at 4 months, and we were told to consider "partial reduction" which we refused. We released Eve to God and trusted Him with her healing. Eve survived the pregnancy, a miracle on its own, but passed on a day later. As heartbroken as we were we could not deny the miracle that occurred as witnessed by my obstetrician at the time.

I had my six weeks check up at the time. The obstetrician who delivered my twins looked at me and said, "I have to tell you something, Nicole. It wasn't looking like you were going to make it. You lost so much blood, and we weren't sure the babies were going to make it either. When I performed the C-section, I saw something. I saw your daughter spooning your son. She had her butt facing me, and she had herself wrapped around your son in a protective stance. If she hadn't done that, your son would have swallowed too much blood and choked on it. I have never seen that before in all my years, especially with a baby in her condition. It was a miracle that you all survived. You are the strongest woman I know". A miracle? I left the office confused. Had I been looking at this all wrong? Yes, I was in agony. My cries wracked my body, tearing at my stitches until I thought I would break, but yet, a miracle?

I couldn't understand it at the time because the pain of loss was just too great, but five years later I can say that in releasing that which was most precious to me, I received His miracle. I so desperately wanted Eve to be healed, but only when I released what I thought God should have done, was I truly able to see the beauty from the ashes of death. I survived and so did Christian. Does this change the pain and grief? No, it doesn't and to pretend otherwise would be dishonest, but it shows the Mighty hand of God in the situation as the role of Protector.

Shortly after the birth I began feeling very ill and was hospitalized. A blood test revealed that due to the trauma of delivery I developed

Secondary Addison's disease, a life threatening disease. I began a daily regimen of steroids and became so ill that I could barely leave the house. The steroids replaced the Cortisol my body would not produce and in doing so lowered my immune system. I was surviving but not thriving. After dealing with my daughter Eve's memorial service and a newborn son this felt like a final blow. I could no longer exercise the way I used to, eat the way I used to, and everything changed. I had to follow a strict diet of supplements and cut out foods that were irritating my stomach due to the steroids. Going out to eat was impossible, and I could not even be around anyone who had a cold. During those years of forced stillness, God used the time to heal me of internal wounds and grief and brought me closer to Him. At my healthiest being still was torture for me. I needed to constantly move and perform. However, God used the stillness to establish my identity, giftings and relationship with Him. Along with that came the struggle of releasing my former life, former clothes that fit, and chronic movement that was ingrained in me. Once releasing those things to Him, my hands were ready to receive the destiny He chose. In prophetic ministry stillness is a requirement. While the Holy Spirit speaks to us anywhere and everywhere we must take time to quietly seek His face and His presence. Having no other choice but to be still for seven years, being grounded, allowed me to grow deeper roots into the Living Water that would sustain me for the next storm. Now, while still on steroids, He is incrementally healing me, and I am no longer housebound. I still need to schedule periodic times of rest and recovery after events, but I am in fellowship again, which is yet something else I have received while releasing,

Still the act of releasing is difficult. It's so much easier to let go of the things that harm us and prevent our spiritual growth but what happens when the thing you are asked to release is the very desire God put in your heart? When we look at Isaiah 43 we see that the verse says, "former things" and "things of old". However those former things and old things don't necessarily mean bad things. My husband Chris and I are experiencing this situation currently as I write this. During our In Vitro process we created five beautiful babies together in the form of embryos. Our hope as a couple had always been to carry another set of our children. After the diagnosis of Addison's the doctor warned that carrying babies again would kill me and I would not survive the pregnancy. Chris and I were blessed to have insurance that paid to keep our babies safe in storage. Once the insurance stopped covering after five years Chris and I were left with a decision. We had prayed for years for my healing to take place. First, so I would be restored and second so we could consider increasing our family. Even after all of the suffering we endured, God planted the desire for another child in my heart. It makes no sense in the natural but there it was. Yet the expiration date was up, I wasn't healed completely, and it was time to decide. God revealed the year before His decision to donate our babies to a Christian agency that allows us to pick a family to bless. Truth be told, I didn't want to hear it and if I am honest today, I am devastated. Could it be that God was asking me to bless another woman with our children? The children Chris and I made? The children that we so desperately prayed for? My children that I want to carry? He is asking Chris and I to do so. I struggled with the decision, and I felt like I was going to vomit every time I thought of it. I had to remind myself that God is God all the time and His character never changes even when circumstances do. I asked Him if we could be blessed with a surrogate and asked those close to me to pray for the same. The answer was "No" confirmed all around. God was indeed asking Chris and I to release our five remaining children we desperately want, Christian's siblings, our future.

This is where that verse in Isaiah becomes less exciting doesn't it? Because those former things and those things of old are not bad things, they are just not a part of this new season. The process that it will take us to fill out the paperwork and pick a family is approximately four to nine months. We know the toll it will take as the process drags out and our hearts break more. It's so important to realize that when God asks us to release something it doesn't mean that what we receive will take away the pain of what we are losing. It's easy to look at what we are receiving as a replacement, but it isn't, it's a new thing. When Job suffered physically and emotionally from illness and losing all of his children the blessing of more children and healing did not change the loss. I feel this is so important to understand so we don't fool ourselves into believing that the grief of what we must release dissipates upon receiving the new thing. The truth is Job still had to recover from the trauma he endured, and that takes time. There is no quick fix as we must till the rocky soil, and let God add new fresh soil to plant the new seeds in. Then we must wait for the seeds to take root and grow all while watering them with His Living Water. The hope and comfort is that what God has for us is good because He is good.

While we are going through this process and it is just the beginning, we know that in releasing our five babies to another family we are emptying our hands of what God says we must. As we lift up our empty hands in grief and worship we have the expectation that they will be filled again with the new thing He has for us. Still restoration does not mean replacement, and we are painfully aware of this. In turn this act of release is answering the prayers of another family. The act of giving away the blessing you so desperately want for yourself is the journey of faith and trust. What is God asking you to release today? Do you trust Him enough with the outcome?

Prayer Starter: Father, I come before you asking you to help me release what is in my hand for the new thing you have for me. It is not easy to release what I hold dear to my heart. It is not easy to release that which I wanted for myself and my family even though I am releasing it to You. Please guide my hand, opening each finger tenderly, and speak softly to me as I release what is no longer my own. In Your Name, Amen.

Healing in the Hem

"And when the men of that place recognized Jesus, they sent word to all the surrounding country. People brought all their sick to him and begged him to let the sick just touch the edge of his cloak, and all who touched it were healed." Matthew 14: 35-36

Yesterday was March 1st, which is simply the start of the month for most people, just not for me. Every four years on Leap Year, my daughter Eve's death day arrives. Even the years when there is no February 29th, my husband and I feel it just the same; the only difference is that we feel it on March 1st. Others have moved on with their lives, five years come and gone, but that day for us still hurts. Each year that goes by I expect it to be different and in some ways it is. It's not like the first year, but it's not like the last year either. They say that there are just some wounds that time will not heal, but I say time was never intended to heal wounds,and the loss of a child is one of those wounds. While God has done intensive and incredible healing in our lives, it doesn't mean we don't grieve. The healing that has occurred is evidenced by the joy we choose rather than the sorrow that we can potentially wallow in. The expectation I have of God is great because He is a great God, but I am still responsible for reaching. When the day of Eve's passing arrives, I am usually poured out from motherhood and life. It seems there is no time to shed my tears or grieve. So I find quiet moments like this morning to lie at His feet and reach for the hem of His garment. It's all I can muster at the moment, but it's enough.

As I was reading Matthew 14, the last two verses struck me hard. I imagined a crowd of people, many sick and suffering, seeking relief. They had no recourse, Jesus was passing through, and they were not going to miss Him. They were hungry and desperate for healing, so desperate that they did not reach Jesus and look Him in the eye, but rather begged to touch the edge of His cloak. The edge of the cloak was known as the fringe. The cloak Jesus wore was fitting for a Jewish man. In Mosaic law, Jewish men were to wear robes with tassels at the edges, in particular, the four corners of the mantle.

"Then the Lord said to Moses, 'Give the following instructions to the people of Israel: Throughout the generations to come, you must make tassels for the hems of your clothing and attach them with a blue cord.When you see the tassels, you will remember and obey all the commands of the Lord instead of following your own desires and defiling yourselves, as you are prone to do. The tassels will help you remember that you must obey all my commands and be holy to your God. I am the Lord your God who brought you out of the land of Egypt that I might be your God. I am the Lord your God!'" Numbers 15:37-41

The tassels on the robes were symbolic of identity, reminding those who wore them that there is a larger grafting taking place and that those who wore them belonged to God, were in covenant with God, and were to obey His commandments. When the sick grabbed the tassels of Jesus's robe, otherwise known as the hem of His garment they were healed because they were identifying with Him. Identifying with whom they knew Him to be. In a crowd of people, who would prostrate themselves on the ground to touch the tassel unless they trusted the One who wore it? This is faith in action! There is a responsibility we have to reach for the fringe of Jesus, to touch the tassel and believe that in doing so we will be changed physically, spiritually, and emotionally. The word fringe also means, "not part of the mainstream" and "unconventional". Here we have a crowd of unconventional outcasts due to infirmity. They are on the fringe of society, often ignored and mistreated. Still, they understand that the healing comes in identifying with Christ, and so they seek their healing where they know they will receive it. These outcasts having no reason to believe that Jesus would even acknowledge them acted in Faith based on who He was. That was enough for them. It's not enough that we seek our healing, but that we also reach out to those who are on the fringes of our society. We must share with others the truth about tassels so that we can be a living example.

When we look at the Pharisees, we see that they wore robes as well with tassels, but there was something much different about the robe Jesus wore and the robes they wore. Jesus referred to this in Matthew 23:5-6 when he said, "Everything they do is done for people to see: They make their phylacteries wide and the tassels on their garments long they love the place of honor at banquets and the most important seats in the synagogues;" The Pharisees had a theological spirit, focusing on their man made teachings and rules rather than the heart. Their tassels were longer to show how religious they were. The phylacteries were scrolls of paper or parchment. Four paragraphs of the law were written out and placed on their foreheads and arms. However, the Pharisees made their phylacteries extra wide to make it more noticeable. While normally phylacteries were worn during prayer, the Pharisees wore them all the time so others would be impressed at their devotion. Have you ever worn your Faith as a badge for all to see rather than an invitation for others to attend? Outwardly, it looked good, but inside the Pharisees were filled with hypocrisy, and their motivations were selfish. Their hearts were hardened, making them impossible to receive Jesus and His teaching. They did not know desperate need as those who were physically ill did. However, the Pharisees experienced a spiritual form of sickness which is so much worse. The Pharisees were no different than those on the fringe of society, for although they were not outcasts in the natural world, they were outcasts in the spiritual realm. The Pharisees' tassels did not hold healing, but condemnation reminding others how Holy they were and how sinful everyone else was. Religion and ritual will never heal you but a relationship with Jesus will.

The key to healing comes when we reach for the fringe of Jesus, identifying with Him, knowing that we are His in every way. Understanding who He is, and who we are in Him is the only way. This is what abiding looks like. Wearing longer tassels and other forms of religious costume will never be true healing because it lacks desperation and hunger. It is a false identity that is subtle in its deception because it seeks to convince us that we lack nothing. How can we receive healing if our vessels are already filled? The Pharisees loved to have places of honor at large events where they could be seen and enjoyed preferential seating. If we are to be healed, we can't be seated at the table of religion; we must come to the point where we are willing to lay down at His feet. It is there where we will find the strength to reach for the source of healing. We must come with expectation and Faith, knowing that there is healing in the hem.

What are you seeking healing for today? I encourage you to stop hiding behind the long tassels of false identity and identify with the one who can heal you.

Prayer Starter: Thank You, Lord that there is healing at the hem of Your garment, and there is peace at Your feet. I thank You, Jesus, that You are the collector of tears, and not one escapes Your notice. I bring before You my grief and my heartache over what I have lost, knowing that You can make beauty from ashes. I lay down by Your feet, touching Your tassel, expecting a deeper healing in You. Thank You for allowing all things, even the most painful, to work together for my good. In Your Precious and Holy Name, Amen.

Disappointment in the Desert

"As for Philip, an angel of the Lord said to him, "Go south[a] down the desert road that runs from Jerusalem to Gaza." So he started out, and he met the treasurer of Ethiopia, a eunuch of great authority under the Kandake, the queen of Ethiopia. The eunuch had gone to Jerusalem to worship, and he was now returning. Seated in his carriage, he was reading aloud from the book of the prophet Isaiah. The Holy Spirit said to Philip, "Go over and walk along beside the carriage." Philip ran over and heard the man reading from the prophet Isaiah. Philip asked, "Do you understand what you are reading?" The man replied, "How can I, unless someone instructs me?" And he urged   Philip to come up into the carriage and sit with him. The passage of Scripture he had been reading was this:

"He was led like a sheep to the slaughter.
And as a lamb is silent before the shearers,
he did not open his mouth.
He was humiliated and received no justice.
Who can speak of his descendants?
For his life was taken from the earth."
The eunuch asked Philip, "Tell me, was the prophet talking about himself or someone else?" So beginning with this same Scripture, Philip told him the Good News about Jesus.
As they rode along, they came to some water, and the eunuch said, "Look! There's some water! Why can't I be baptized?" He ordered the carriage to stop, and they went down into the water, and Philip baptized him.
When they came up out of the water, the Spirit of the Lord snatched Philip away. The eunuch never saw him again but went on his way rejoicing. Meanwhile, Philip found himself farther north at the town of Azotus. He preached the Good News there and in every town along the way until he came to Caesarea."
Acts 8: 26- 40 (NLT)

I have read the account of Philip before, and this passage always intrigued me.This Philip was not the apostle Philip but one of the seven organizers of food distribution in the early church. In his obedience to God, Philip spread the good news preaching the gospel as Jesus instructed. In fact, Philip was one of the first to heed this command. Philip was on fire, preaching the gospel to the Samaritans. He had a successful ministry with great crowds lined up to hear this message of salvation. It was at this pinnacle of success that the Lord told Philip through an angel to travel down a desert road. That desert road was to lead Philip to his next assignment, and he obeyed the Word of the Lord. Such obedience led Philip to catch up to a carriage where a eunuch was reading Isaiah but did not understand the meaning of what he was reading. Philip started a discussion asking the man if he wanted help interpreting what the Scripture was saying. The man accepted Jesus and asked Philip to baptize him. Once the man was baptized, the Holy Spirit lifted Philip up and carried him away to his next assignment.

I admire Philip in this passage because he didn't stop and ask questions or complain. He didn't ask the angel for an autograph. He didn't ask the Spirit to confirm it fifty times to be sure. The fact that Philip was not phased at all tells us that he was used to walking in the supernatural. It was a way of life. Many of us want such experiences but are we willing to endure the journey it takes to live a supernatural lifestyle?

When we look at Philip's reaction to this new assignment we see obedience in action. Have you ever been doing what God has called you to do and then He changes the assignment? I have. In this season many things are on pause as I heed the voice of His Spirit. Looking through the lens of the world, it doesn't make any sense. Naturally if something is successful you keep doing it, you don't stop. But this isn't the natural we are dealing with; it is the supernatural, and we are designed for supernatural experiences with the Holy Spirit. Often these encounters do not make sense, they do not feel comfortable, and they cannot be contained, they just are. Our job is to accept and obey like Philip. I admire Philip because he did not question or complain but he was obedient and accepted what appeared like a demotion to follow the Spirit of God. It wasn't practical, but it's not supposed to be.

When Philip saw the assignment waiting for him, he did not flinch he focused. He walked down the desert road and obeyed the Holy Spirit's command to walk beside the carriage. Philip left a multitude to go after the one man. Does this make sense in the natural? Preaching to multitudes surely would create more conversions than one eunuch in a carriage, right? Only God knew who this eunuch was. He was a high ranking treasurer and served the Queen of Ethiopia. By starting a conversation, Phlip was able to instruct the man on what he was reading, preaching the good news of Jesus. In doing so, Philip revealed his heart was for the one lost sheep just as it was for the many. To Philip the audience didn't matter, the platform didn't matter, the message mattered. The treasurer became so excited that he accepted the gift of salvation and asked Philip to baptize him and went on his way rejoicing. It wasn't one man though was it? This man had a position of authority and the ear of the Queen. He was a changed man and would open the door of the gospel to an entire country. Philip didn't know this at the time, but did it matter? No. The heart of Jesus was evident in Philip in that he focused on this man rather than the multitude.

Once Philip completed the assignment, he didn't have to trek back on the wilderness road. The Spirit of God carried him to his next assignment representing acceleration. When we are in those desert places, it doesn't feel like a supernatural assignment but I assure you it is. We are being sanctified and prepared for our next assignment. I am speaking to someone today as I write this including myself that what feels like a demotion is not. It is a molding from the Master Potter, for you have shown that you are faithful. This is not a punishment but a promotion. This feels like a destination, but it's just a drive through. When you are faithful in the desert, His Spirit will accelerate you to the crux of your call. You were designed with a purpose, even though you feel directionless. Walk the road like Philip, and see what you are to learn in this season. Don't waste the moments in between the desert and the destination.

Prayer Starter: Lord, even though I may not like what You have for me today, I know that this today is necessary for my tomorrow. Give me the strength and wisdom to discern what You are teaching me in this particular season of my life. I want no lesson wasted, Lord.

Fill me with Your presence, instruction, and direction. Comfort me when the road is long, and carry me when it is time to move on. Remind me, Lord, when I become discouraged that this desert is not my destination. Thank You for Your faithfulness, Lord. In Your Name, I pray, Amen.

Walking in the Wilderness

When I hear the words wilderness and desert, I picture a dry and barren land where nothing can grow. It's a place where I imagine sand dunes for miles, so dry where there is chronic thirst, but no water. I imagine the drudgery of traveling such a place even if it is just a passing through. It seems lonely because it is. As I am writing this today, I am in that place. I am in that wilderness, that parched place where my life and the meaning that I gave it is gone. Everything I once held dear has been placed on hold, paused in this season, while the Holy Spirit takes me through the desert, known as the "dark night of the soul". In the desert is where the deeper level of healing begins. It's easy to ignore your thirst in the middle of the day when a faucet is only a few feet away. When all you see is sand, and all you feel is heat, you become acutely aware of your desperate need for water. In this season God is showing me keys to surviving the wilderness.

"The wilderness and the solitary place shall be glad for them; and the desert shall rejoice, and blossom as the rose." Isaiah 35:1 Walking in the Wilderness requires acceptance and perseverance.

God uses the wilderness seasons of our lives to manifest Himself in the greatest of ways. As we wearily travel the desolate land of our wilderness, He plants Himself as the Living Well. We who are parched and weary, feeling isolated, can be refilled even in the wilderness. In Isaiah 35:1, the prophet is describing a wilderness who is rejoicing and then blossoming, going against its very nature. How can there be joy in a place of desolation? When we are in a spiritual desert, it is entirely possible to find joy everlasting. Even in a desolate season joy can be found, thus changing the climate of the desert, allowing life to bloom as the rose. The environment of the desert will not change on its own, but when we accept that we are to settle there for a while, we can change the climate. Our presence in a place where nothing seems to grow is when the Holy Spirit does the most work, once again proving His Holy power in growing something out of what appears lifeless.

"About this time another large crowd had gathered, and the people ran out of food again. Jesus called his disciples and told them, 'I feel sorry for these people. They have been here with me for three days, and they have nothing left to eat. If I send them home hungry, they will faint along the way. For some of them have come a long distance.' His disciples replied, 'How are we supposed to find enough food to feed them out here in the wilderness?' Jesus

asked, 'How much bread do you have?' 'Seven loaves', they replied." Mark 8:1-5

2. Wisdom in the wilderness requires giving all that you have over to Him and reaching for all that He has for you.

The disciples noticed that they were in an environment where there was nothing. They recognized that the crowds were not going to get fed based on the area where Jesus spoke. Instead of depending on the environment to provide for them, Jesus asked for what they already had. When in a wilderness season, we cry out to God asking Him to provide for us but rarely do we say to Him, "This is all I have left, but you can have it." Self-preservation in a desolate area is a natural instinct, but we are to bypass that instinct so that God can multiply what we are bringing to Him. When Jesus was handed the loaves of bread, He multiplied it, but not all at once. The crowd was large, but He did not make a mountain of bread for all to see. Instead, only as the individuals took their fill, more was multiplied. It was clear that no bread was to be found in the desert, but making a mountain of bread and fish would have allowed the crowd to see abundance and be comforted by it. The action of Faith is where they stuck their hand in the basket, trusting that there was something to be had. When we are in a place of feeling stripped and bare, we always have something to give, and in giving what we have to God, we trust that He will multiply it and that as we reach for it, we will be filled.

"And great crowds came together to hear and to be healed by Him of their infirmities. But He withdrew to the wilderness and prayed." Luke 5:15-16

3. Willingly withdrawing into the wilderness requires maturity.

While we are not meant to live in the wilderness, once we are released, we mustn't abandon it forever. The wilderness, while not habitable, is a place where we can be recharged and renewed. It is a place where we can learn to withdraw from the distractions of our world and of our lives, our thoughts and be filled. We can use the barren environment to our advantage, seeking the only source of Living Water that exists. Willingly withdrawing requires maturity. So few are willing to give up their everyday distractions and busyness to retreat into the desert land. Jesus chose the wilderness to withdraw because He understood that He needed to be filled in order to pour out. He knew that the crowds, their needs would press in on Him making it too distracting to focus on His Father. Other voices would chime in disrupting His quiet time. As women, I feel this is an important message because very rarely do we perceive it's okay to withdraw from our families to have quiet time with the Lord. I remember feeling the constant pull of motherhood, being a wife, business owner, and more. The needs were overflowing, but my tank was empty. We are called to withdraw from the chaos of our world, whatever it may look like, and spend time alone in our wilderness with His Spirit. This isn't selfish, it's essential. Without this, we will not be able to pour out in our everyday lives. Whether you work on the outside of the home or inside of the home, whether you have one child or many children, whether you are in ministry or attend ministry, our power comes from our intimacy with Him.

The wilderness is not a fun place to be, but it is useful. At first, we may resent it, but the lessons we learn from it are eternal. Jesus showed us that multiplication can occur in the wilderness and that while solitary, it is a good place to be filled.

What is your wilderness? What is God teaching you through your visit there?

Prayer Starter: Lord, we thank you for the wilderness we are in. Teach us to find joy in the dry and barren places of our lives. Allow us to drink from Your Living streams so we may be replenished and persevere. We bring You all of us, Lord, We bring all of the broken pieces and hold on to nothing but You. Teach us how to be held in this moment, Lord. In Your Name, we pray, Amen.

Walking in Weariness

"The Lᴏʀᴅ said, 'Go out and stand on the mountain in the presence of the Lᴏʀᴅ, for the Lᴏʀᴅ is about to pass by'."

"Then a great and powerful wind tore the mountains apart and shattered the rocks before the Lᴏʀᴅ, but the Lᴏʀᴅ was not in the wind. After the wind there was an earthquake, but the Lᴏʀᴅ was not in the earthquake. After the earthquake came a fire, but the Lᴏʀᴅ was not in the fire. And after the fire came a gentle whisper. When Elijah heard it, he pulled his cloak over his face and went out and stood at the mouth of the cave." 1 Kings 11-13

I was finishing up my devotional when I saw the bible verse of the day pop up on my phone, 1Kings 19: 11-13. Despite all of the ways God could have revealed Himself, he showed up in a whisper. This led me to re-read 1 Kings 18 and then 19.

Elijah as God's Vessel

In 1 Kings 18, Elijah is coming off of a powerful victory. During a time when God's prophets were being murdered by Jezebel, the Israelites had turned away from God worshiping Baal instead. In obedience, Elijah presented himself to Ahab and created a challenge to the people: "I am the only one of the Lord's prophets left, but Baal has four hundred and fifty prophets. Get two bulls for us. Let Baal's prophets choose one for themselves, and let them cut it into pieces and put it on the wood but not set fire to it. I will prepare the other bull and put it on the wood but not set fire to it. Then you call on the name of your god, and I will call on the name of the Lord. The god who answers by fire—he is God." 1 Kings 18:22-24 The people agreed to this.

God showed up in a big way bringing fire to a water entrenched altar, burning up the water, the sacrifice, and even the stones and soil. The Israelites turned their hearts back to God, claiming Him as the One True God. Imagine the faith it took in God, during a drought for Elijah to command the precious commodity of water to be used on an altar. Elijah was so certain that God was going to come through. Elijah then killed all of Baal's prophets and the drought ended. Directly after it began to rain, God gave Elijah the strength to run on foot to the town of Jezreel. Throughout the process, Elijah acted in obedience to God only doing as He directed.

However, once Ahab reiterated what happened to Jezebel things took a turn for the worse. In 1 Kings 19:1, Ahab twists the truth the way one who is hard hearted would. He attributes the actions of Elijah to be of Elijah's doing as opposed to God's doing. Ahab refused to give God credit. 1 Kings 19: 1 states, "Now Ahab told Jezebel everything Elijah had done and how he had killed all the prophets with the sword."

In verse 2, "So Jezebel sent a messenger to Elijah to say, "May the gods deal with me, be it ever so severely if by this time tomorrow I do not make your life like that of one of them." Jezebel makes a threat to Elijah putting a contract out on his life, which sends him running to the wilderness and asking God to take his life.

Why Did Elijah Become Defeated?

Elijah, a great man of God, used by God as His mighty vessel ran away and lost his will to live. Elijah was physically and spiritually exhausted from the warfare he was engaged in. He came to a broom bush, sat down under it and prayed that he might die. In 1 Kings 19:4, Elijah says, "I have had enough, Lord," he said. "Take my life; I am no better than my ancestors."

There are many times when Christian warriors have faced the battlefield and become weary from the fight, but in this instance, Elijah had let this threat consume him. He did not ask God if he should flee to the wilderness, or seek His counsel on the next move. He was so devastated by this threat that he hid, and even asked God to take his life. After God showed such a Mighty display of power you would think Elijah would be more confident, but yet he wasn't. He was human. If such a prophet as Elijah can become discouraged, it is no wonder that we can become weary and discouraged as well.

We can use Elijah's example to see where human patterns come in. Even though Elijah was God's vessel and saw God use him to end a drought, stand up against Jezebel and Ahab, and ran 20 miles to Jezreel on foot, he had a moment in time where he felt completely defeated by his Enemy and weary as well. When we are in those moments of defeat, it is so easy to make bad choices using our emotions rather than listening to God's voice.

It started with Elijah having an expectation about how God was going to move. Defeat only exists when we expect a certain outcome. Rather than allowing God to decide what it looks like or how our situation will play out, we have an expectation. When that expectation is not met, we become utterly disappointed and begin to feel defeated. While God's display of power in front of the Israelites was a victory, it did not turn out the way Elijah expected. If it had, then he would not have slipped into the slope of defeat strong enough to end his life. Elijah certainly didn't envision things becoming WORSE after he obeyed God. Fear gripped Elijah in those moments and left him wiped out and relying on his strength. He asked God before falling asleep to end his life. What if we responded by expecting God to move but just released the conditional way we want Him to move?

How did God Respond?

While Elijah responded in his human strength, God responded in the way a loving Father would: He nursed Elijah until he was rejuvenated.

1.God sent an angel to minister to his physical needs. God did not engage Elijah in conversation about his shortcomings but fed him twice. 1 Kings 19: 5-9 states,
"All at once an angel touched him and said, "Get up and eat." He looked around, and there by his head was some bread baked over hot coals, and a jar of water. He ate and drank and then lay down again.The angel of the Lord came back a second time and touched him and said, "Get up and eat, for the journey is too much for you." So he got up and ate and drank. Strengthened by that food, he traveled forty days and forty nights until he reached Horeb, the mountain of God. There he went into a cave and spent the night."

2. God appeared to Elijah with a question, "What are you doing here, Elijah." I love this in particular because as God He already knows, but our God is a relational God and is opening up a dialogue with His prophet. God is a God of intimacy and love. Elijah was still in the cave at this point.

3. God gently calls Elijah out of the cave telling him to come on the mountain top to experience His presence, but Elijah stays in the cave.

4. God reminds Elijah of His Holy power and His gentle Love through a whisper in 1 KIngs 19: 11- 13,"Then a great and powerful wind tore the mountains apart and shattered the rocks before the Lord, but the Lord was not in the wind. After the wind, there was an earthquake, but the Lord was not in the earthquake. After the earthquake came a fire, but the Lord was not in the fire. And after the fire came a gentle whisper." When Elijah heard it, he pulled his

cloak over his face and went out and stood at the mouth of the cave.

5. God initiates conversation with Elijah again giving him the opportunity to vent his frustrations in His Holy presence not in hiding, which he does.

6. God gives Elijah clear instructions on how to proceed, allowing Elijah, a successor in Elisha.

God did not punish or condemn Elijah for his momentary weakness and weariness. He understood Elijah's needs and ministered to him. He knew that Elijah's heart was weary and compassionately and tenderly tended those needs. It's so easy to question our Faith when we feel defeated or weary, but we serve a God who will minister to us in His still small voice through the Holy Spirit. In turn, we must respond in obedience. We too should respond the way God did to Elijah. When we encounter the brokenhearted and the weary soldiers, do we tell them to have more faith or do we minister to them? Are we compassionate and tender in our response to our fellow soldiers who are struggling and under enemy attack? This portion of scripture is a great reminder to trust and obey God even through trials and tribulations, but God's response to Elijah is a phenomenal example of how to respond to fellow brothers and sisters in Christ who are suffering as well.

Prayer Starter: Lord, the battle is long, and my strength feels like it's in short supply, I want just to run and hide in my cave rather than face the false accusations and threats against me. Instead, Lord, give me the strength to run to you rather than following my feelings. I want to live a life of obedience no matter what the cost. I thank You, Lord, for being so tender when I am weary. Thank you for nurturing me back to health spiritually, physically and emotionally. I thank You that You are a God that meets all of my needs. In Jesus' name, I pray, Amen.

Settled on Staying

"The LORD told Joshua, "Today I will begin to make you a great leader in the eyes of all the Israelites. They will know that I am with you, just as I was with Moses. Give this command to the priests who carry the Ark of the Covenant: 'When you reach the banks of the Jordan River, take a few steps into the river and stop there.'"

So Joshua told the Israelites, "Come and listen to what the LORD your God says. Today you will know that the living God is among you. He will surely drive out the Canaanites, Hittites, Hivites,

Perizzites, Girgashites, Amorites, and Jebusites ahead of you. Look, the Ark of the Covenant, which belongs to the Lord of the

whole earth, will lead you across the Jordan River! Now choose twelve men from the tribes of Israel, one from each tribe. The priests will carry the Ark of the LORD, the Lord of all the earth. As soon as their feet touch the water, the flow of water will be cut off upstream, and the river will stand up like a wall."

"So the people left their camp to cross the Jordan, and the priests who were carrying the Ark of the Covenant went ahead of them. It was the harvest season, and the Jordan was overflowing its banks. But as soon as the feet of the priests who were carrying the Ark touched the water at the river's edge, the water above that point began backing up a great distance away at a town called Adam, which is near Zarethan. And the water below that point flowed on to the Dead Sea until the riverbed was dry. Then all the people crossed over near the town of Jericho." Joshua 3:7-16

In my devotional time, the Holy Spirit impressed upon my heart the difference between being still and staying still. To set the premise, Joshua and the Israelites were just about to cross over the Jordan to the Promised Land. They were eager but before even moving Joshua gathered the people to hear the Word of the Lord. Remember that they had fought and conquered many enemies after being encamped at Shittim for many months. Then they moved to another encampment only six or seven miles from the Jordan river, and there they stayed for three days. Joshua 3:1 is where after camping for only three days they were asked to move again this time crossing the Jordan. I was thinking about this part for a while and wondered why they'd be asked to move such a short distance. I thought that it would be so much more efficient if they just moved from Shittim to Jordan right? Wrong. When we are in a place of staying still for a while, it's easy to forget the destiny God has for us. The Israelites became used to sedentary camp life. Yes, they knew the promises of God and believed them but in the process of waiting routines were established. Moving the Israelites for only a few days reestablished the plans and purposes God had for their lives. It reminded the Israelites that they were a transient community and that the place where they had stayed for many months and possibly even years was not their destination. There is such a difference between being still and staying still. Being is a state of existence or a state of living, but staying is "to remain in the same place or remain in a specified place or position." There are times when God asks us to be still and to stay still, but many times we end up staying longer than we should. We become accustomed and comfortable with the circumstances even if they are painful. When that happens, it can be easy to miss when God calls us to move.

I recently experienced this myself, when after dealing with the grief of donating our babies to bless another family. It was okay to grieve and be still in His presence, but that turned into me staying curled up in an emotional ball unwilling to move. Being still turned into staying still until the Holy Spirit gently nudged me and said, it's time to pick up your camp and move forward. He was not telling me to hurry up and move on, but He was reminding me that emotional paralysis was beginning to occur the longer I stayed in the horizontal position. The same happens with muscles that are not used; they begin to atrophy. So there are times when we need to be still and even stay there for a little bit but always with the intention of moving forward. Nothing good comes from remaining in a specified position too long by our hand.

Before crossing the Jordan, it was important for the Israelites to be still and hear the Word of the Lord. After being stationary for so long, they were most likely anxious to move on. When we are feeling stuck or stationary in an area of our lives, it is so easy to rush ahead to the promises of God. During the transitioning period from wandering the wilderness to the presence of promise, it is more important than ever to be sure footed which can only happen with the Word and presence of the Living God. After hearing the Word of the Lord, they proceeded in obedience.

Before the miracle happened the priests first, while holding the Ark of the Lord, had to take a step. The waters would not part unless the priests placed their feet in the water. Faith was required for the miracle to take place. What if the priests were afraid? What if they couldn't deal with the thought of drowning? Staying in this instance would be disobedience. Staying still would not get them across, but a move of Faith did. As the priests placed their fear aside and their feet in front God performed the miracle and the water backed away until the riverbed was dry.

It can be so confusing to know when to stay still and when to move but when we enter His presence we discern His voice, and He tells us how to proceed. Psalm 46:10 instructs us to "Be still and know that He is God," which we will never know if we don't come before Him. Entering into His presence is where revelation is found! So many times I have watched while people just stay still waiting for God to open the door when He is calling them to take a step of Faith. Many times I have been that person so paralyzed by the fear of making a mistake that I just don't move at all; waiting for an invitation that I have already received. It can happen to any of us, but when we are in His presence, His perfect peace comes over us and clarity begins to chip away at the confusion and chaos within our minds.

How to Discern Staying and Moving

1. Is there fear associated with moving forward? For me, I was a former "take matters into your own hands" kind of girl. Over the decades I moved to the opposite end of the spectrum. What I felt was patience was really paralysis. Fear made me stay, and rather than taking that step of Faith I

wondered if I was forcing a door open. God is not a tightrope God, and He doesn't give Himself in pieces. He is a good God and a Good Father. Be still in His presence and ask Him, and if you discern that fear is holding you back move forward in Faith.

2. Is this a season? There are seasons in the wilderness, and while you are moving forward in maturity, it can feel like you are staying still. The truth is that you have done nothing wrong! If you are in a wilderness season you are in training, so don't try to move out of a season of preparation. Still, move as He tells you to but also accepts that this season is where you will stay for a time until He releases you.

3. Is this surgery? I am currently in the last parts of this season where He is cutting out the wounds and grief that loss and circumstances have caused. He is binding those wounds and pouring the balm of Gilead over them. This is not the time to move! Just like a real surgery moving will do more harm than good. It hurts, I know, and your instinct is to move forward to the Promised Land. I get it. The problem is if you move you will need more surgery and recovery will be harder. This is a time to be perfectly still. Stay still and be still trusting that He will do what He promised and you are not missing out or being punished but rather promoted. Even the priests had to be consecrated before carrying the Ark. They also had to stay still after taking a step holding the Ark while everyone else passed. Have you ever felt like that? Everyone seems to be passing by you heading towards their Promise Land, but there you are stuck in the riverbed of unrest? There is a purpose to this pain, and many times our surgery season is a testimony and blessing to others. It doesn't feel important, but it is.

4. Are you impatient? Is what you are calling Faith really just you trying to manufacture something that God should be cultivating instead? When I was in my early twenties, I

received a prophetic word about having an entrepreneurial gift. I was a teacher at the time, and just finished my Master's degree. As soon as that Word hit my hands, I created a business model for a tutoring site. It was a great model, but I didn't consult God on the matter. I just ran ahead and did what I wanted to do. A week later I fell ill, and afterward, I asked God about whether I should begin to implement this plan. He said no, it was not the time and Education was not the field He was referring to. All of those hours I wasted trying to put my spin on His prophetic Word. Now, nearly twenty years later I see how important it is to pray over the prophetic word and be still listening to God and waiting for Him to guide in the fulfillment of His promise. He has been showing me how this gift will be used and it's nothing I would have ever seen all those years ago. We can cultivate His promises through prayer and intercession, but running forward in our own strength is foolish.

It can be confusing to know when to stay and when to move, but the intent of our hearts always reveal the true nature. Not moving when we should look Holy as we "wait for God to open the door" but moving forward and calling it Faith is also a way to fool ourselves and feed our flesh. Every transition and every season calls for being still in His presence, of that we are certain. When we are filled with His presence, wisdom comes from the overflow, and that's a good place to set up camp.

Prayer Starter: Lord, in this time, please give me the clarity to see through Your eyes. I don't want to move without Your guidance. Help me to be still in Your presence so that I can receive divine wisdom, so I don't make a move without Your blessing. In Your Name, Amen.

Running on Empty

"And to know this love that surpasses knowledge--that you may be filled to the measure of all the fullness of God." NIV Ephesians 3:19

I have so many tanks you would think I am in the automotive industry. I have a love tank, an energy tank, and a spiritual tank. So many times I am running on empty in the love and energy arena, but I notice my ability to cope and handle the emptiness is dependent on my spiritual tank. When the wounds of life and circumstances threaten to overwhelm me my instinct is to move faster rather than be still. The faster I move, the more I accomplish giving me a measurable outcome amidst the chaos of circumstances I cannot control. I wonder what would happen if a cup that needed to be filled moved around constantly. Sure, it may get a splash of water in here and there, but it would remain mostly empty. I am in that surgery season where the Holy Spirit is dealing with the wounds that come from circumstances beyond my control. He gave me a waking vision the other day. I was on a surgery table, and I was "open" while God was performing surgery and Jesus was holding my hand. I sensed the comfort of the Holy Spirit there as well. I was trying to get up and asking God if the surgery was over so I could go to Physical therapy and heal. He kept showing me that trying to move during surgery is counterproductive. It only makes matters worse and in fact is contrary to the whole purpose of the surgery. In fact moving around during surgery would most likely require MORE surgery!

We are at stage four of our embryo adoption, where God asked us to donate five of our fully developed beautiful children (embryos) to another family. We want to keep our babies, but God does not want us to, and although I was praying for the healing that would allow me to carry them, it is not His will. He led us to a wonderful Christian agency called Snowflakes. I love that they treat our embryos like the babies they are, taking us through the adoption process and allowing us to choose the family to raise our babies. I am not blind to the blessing, but honestly, the only thing I feel filled with lately is tears, not power. The layers of grief I am experiencing is incredible over the last few months. The emptiness makes me feel helpless, as I look at my five-year-old son playing by himself and remember how our family had to get through the loss of his twin after childbirth. Those five babies though, they were the hope that I'd be in a place to carry a few more. They were the measure of my motherhood fullness, and they shouldn't have been. My measure and my fullness should be Him and Him alone. This is not to say we cannot have desires and dreams for our lives, but after losing Eve, I felt that God would not ask me to give away five children that I so desperately want. I felt it would be cruel. And so the loss of Eve became a false insurance policy that He would never ask me to hurt in this area again. That I would never experience the sense of devastation and loss that I felt before and am feeling right now.

Fullness. It's possible to be filled with grief and joy simultaneously. When I think about Jesus right before He endured the cross I am reminded that He too was filled with grief in Matthew 26:38 "Then he said to them, "My soul is overwhelmed with sorrow to the point of death. Stay here and keep watch with me." Jesus knew what pain He would have to endure, and it grieved Him especially as He watched each event unfold before Him. When Eve died after one day, our grieving happened right away and took years to unfold layer by layer. This is different in that the process is taking months. I liken it to a bandaid being ripped off very slowly. As each event unfolds and brings us closer to choosing another family to raise our children there is sorrow that is so overwhelming I often wonder how I can inhale. Despite this agonizing pain, the Word of God says in Hebrews 12:1, ..."For the joy set before him, he endured the cross, scorning its shame, and sat down at the right hand of the throne of God." When I read that I am compelled to pause and reread because the word "joy" seems out of place when we understand the torture that Jesus experienced and endured for our sake. The joy was not experienced during the cross as it was "set before" Him. I can't help but think of a table set with a feast. The starving soul looks longingly still feeling the pain of the hunger pangs, the weakness and faintness within the body, and the strong desire to eat something, anything to make it go away. The joy is that through endurance and perseverance after the trial that starving soul will feast at the table. The joy is knowing with certainty that there is a seat with his name on it. Jesus experienced joy knowing that what was waiting on the other side of this turmoil. Still, the joy set before Him was His accomplished purpose: Defeating Death, Defeating Satan, the Glory of His crown and position at the right hand of the Father. All brought about by obedience.

When we are filled with the measure of the fullness of God our spirit recognizes it and is activated. It comes alive, and it overflows into the wounds creating a sustainable salve that heals the wounds as it rushes over them. This is what makes it possible to experience joy amidst grief. This is the catalyst to obedience when our flesh cries out "take this cup from me!".

The word fullness occurs 12 times in the Bible, but the most incredible verse is Mark 2:21 where the Greek Word fullness is used describing cloth.

"The meaning of the words is this: An old garment, if it be torn, should be mended by a patch of old material; for if a patch of new material is used, its strength or fullness takes away from the old garment to which it is sewn; the old and the new do not agree, the new drags the old and tears it, and so a worse rent is made."

This is why we can't put new wine in old wine skins and it's why old, and new can't cohabitate. When we die to the flesh, we are a new creature in Christ. The old and the new can't be in the same vicinity. The old is always ruined by the new because it cannot contain or sustain it.

In a season of grieving, when I try to find fullness anywhere other than Christ I will remain empty even if the things I desire are good things. All good things can become idols if we are looking to feast on them using them to fill a need only Christ can fill. Only in Him can I be full. When I ponder the fullness of His love, I see that what He is asking of me and my family is not cruel although it feels that way. A loving God cannot be a cruel God. When I put aside my own perception of Christ based on circumstances for the fullness of His perfect love my spirit man becomes full. It's when I try to mix my perception of God with the truth of the Bible that things go wrong. Fleeting perspectives and perceptions never lead us to God but away from Him. He is our portion forever so how can we be full apart from Him?

As we walk through this season of grieving, I am reminded that I must be still in His presence, and for the joy set before me release that which we made into His hands so we may receive that which He has for us instead.

Have you ever had to release something dear to you? How has God ministered to you through that season?

Prayer Starter: Lord, if I am honest, my flesh will not release this to You without a fight. I bind fear, anxiety, and stress associated with releasing this in obedience and loose Faith and Peace over my spirit, mind, soul, heart and body. Give me the strength to endure this place of grief when every part of me wants to run away. Help me to be still and rest in Your Presence where I may be filled to overflowing and heal. I thank You, Lord, for what You have for me and I receive the gift of Your joy today. In Your Holy Name, Amen.

Patience Through the Process

" Now I say to you that you are Peter (which means 'rock'),[a] and upon this rock, I will build my church, and all the powers of hell[b] will not conquer it." Matthew 16:18

I was spending time in the Word this morning and was led to read Matthew 16:18. I always loved the power of this verse. Jesus gives Peter a new name and defies the Enemy at the same time. It's a scripture that always gets me pumped. So, when I felt led to read it again, I was not sure why until it was revealed.

When Simon Peter was given a new name, He was given a new identity. Jesus named Simon, Peter which means "Rock". What struck me the most was that after given a new name, Peter made some of the biggest mistakes. A few verses after Peter was given his new name, we see the impulsive side of him. When Jesus began speaking on the things He would suffer, Peter took Jesus aside and began to reprimand Him until Jesus said in Matthew 16:23, "Jesus turned to Peter and said, 'Get away from me Satan! You are a dangerous trap to me. You are seeing things merely from a human point of view, not from God's.'" Peter's fear of losing Jesus overtook him and instead of supporting Jesus, he made a fool of himself by reprimanding the Messiah!

In John 18:10 when it was time for Jesus to fulfill His destiny, Peter once again, afraid, reacted, "Then Simon Peter drew a sword and slashed off the right ear of Malchus, the high priest's slave." Jesus put a stop to Peter's impulsive behavior by reminding him of His destiny, the cup from which He must drink. Despite Peter's attempts to prevent Jesus from dying, when Jesus finally was arrested and taken, in fear, Peter denied Jesus three times as predicted in Matthew 26:75, " Suddenly, Jesus' words flashed through Peter's mind: 'Before the rooster crows, you will deny three times that you even know me.' And he went away, weeping bitterly."

So, why am I pointing out some of Peter's biggest failures? I am trying to show you that Jesus renamed Peter with a name that had nothing to do with his behavior in the present circumstance but rather who he would become. Peter was impulsive, driven by fear, and stubborn. He spoke and acted before thinking based on what he felt, rather than what Jesus wanted. Peter hardly seems like a rock in these verses. He seems more like a ship tossed to and fro by the storms of life, unstable and unreliable. Rock? I don't think so. Not yet anyway.

Peter was given a new name before his character measured up. This is the role of Jesus operating in the prophetic. Little did Peter know what the future would hold and the process it would take to get there. The journey was long and treacherous for Peter. When God promises us something through prophecy or a Word spoken over us in the present, it may be for this season, but I have found many times it applies to the next season of my life.

While the identity of "Rock" did not fit Peter when faced with pressure during Jesus's life, after Jesus's death Peter learned from his mistakes and walked into his new identity. Peter became a rock, and in writing 1 Peter encouraged persecuted believers all over while himself proclaiming the good news. Peter also wrote 2 Peter, a letter of warning from the mature apostle to be wary of internal attack in the Christian walk such as complacency, stagnancy, false teachers, and more. A few years after writing his second letter, Peter was captured and crucified under the cruel leadership of Nero. The same man who rejected Jesus, left Him at his most vulnerable hour, and attempted to interfere with Jesus's destiny, became the man Jesus said He would become.

The point is that Jesus knew who Peter was before Peter knew just like Jesus knows who we are, even when we don't. When Jesus looks at us, He sees who we truly are and who we are meant to become. Peter didn't automatically change as soon as his identity was revealed. He did not automatically BECOME a rock after it was spoken over him. Peter had to endure his mistakes including denying his best friend at the lowest point. Peter had to suffer through his mistakes, and through the fire, became the man he was told he would be.

I can easily become discouraged when God's promises connected to my destiny, identity, and purpose seem miles away. I begin to resent the season I am in wondering why I am not there yet. I look at the obstacles in my life as a stumbling block rather than a refining tool. What if those very obstacles that I want to bypass are the very tools needed to open the door to my destiny? What if the pressure applied today is the release to my tomorrow? The key to maintaining your strength on this journey from the present to the Promise is patience through the process.

Prayer Starter: Lord Jesus when I look at myself I see all that is wrong with me. Help me see myself through Your eyes. Let me see who You have made me to be and embrace it. Lord, I come before You with all of my mistakes and flaws and bring You my painful circumstances. I drop them at Your feet, Lord, knowing that You will use them to refine me. I pick up instead my new identity in You, knowing that You never make a mistake. Knowing that I am who YOU SAY I am. Grant me patience, O, Lord, as you walk me through this refining process and give me the strength to persevere through You. In Your Precious Name, Amen and Amen.

Dear Reader,

I pray that this devotional book touched your heart. I pray that you were held by Father God as you read it and comforted by the Holy Spirit. I pray Jesus poured the Balm of Gilead in each and every wound you carry. If you would like to leave feedback online I would greatly appreciate it. If you look to be encouraged you can find me at thebridalcall.org and @thebridalcall on Facebook. Be encouraged because the Lord makes beauty from ashes and I am living proof of His Goodness.

Sincerely,
Nicole L Cagna
thebridalcallministries@gmail.com

Made in the USA
Columbia, SC
14 October 2024

44314408R10074